TWO DUDES, ONE PAN

TWO DUDES, ONE PAN

MAXIMUM FLAVOR *from a* Minimalist Kitchen

JON SHOOK *and* VINNY DOTOLO

and RAQUEL PELZEL

PHOTOGRAPHS *BY* KATHRYN RUSSELL

CLARKSON POTTER/PUBLISHERS
NEW YORK

Copyright © 2008 by
JON SHOOK AND VINNY DOTOLO

Photographs copyright © 2008 by
KATHRYN RUSSELL

Published in the United States by
CLARKSON POTTER/PUBLISHERS,
an imprint of the
CROWN PUBLISHING GROUP,
a division of RANDOM HOUSE, INC.,
NEW YORK.

www.crownpublishing.com
www.clarksonpotter.com

CLARKSON N. POTTER is a trademark and POTTER and colophon
are registered trademarks of RANDOM HOUSE, INC.

Library of Congress Cataloging-in-Publication Data

Shook, Jon.
Two dudes, one pan: maximum flavor from a minimalist kitchen/ Jon Shook and Vinny
Dotolo.—1st ed.
1. One-dish meals. I. Dotolo, Vinny. II. Title. III. Title: Two dudes, one pan
TX840.O53S36 2008
641.8'2—dc22   2007040942

978-0-307-38260-3

PRINTED IN CHINA

DESIGN BY JENNIFER K. BEAL DAVIS

10 9 8 7 6 5 4 3 2 1

FIRST EDITION

TO ALL OF our

FAMILIES,

our FRIENDS,

AND MOST OF ALL

our PARENTS,

WHO SUPPORTED US

FROM the START

CONTENTS

INTRODUCTION

Jon: We started our catering company, Carmelized Productions, in 2003 with a pickup truck, a couple of knives, and two pans. Even though our equipment, time, and budget were always limited, we'd always pull off great food for parties of anywhere from ten to two hundred people.

VINNY: We never really planned on becoming caterers. Before we set up our business, we were on the steady track typical of most chefs. We were saving our money to travel through Europe and maybe *stage* (chef speak for apprenticing) at some world-renown-type places. But the catering business took off, and we realized that we had an amazing opportunity to be our own bosses. I was twenty-two years old and Jonny was twenty-one.

Jon: We had this total professional chef background from working in really high-end restaurants like the Strand in South Beach, Florida; the Wildflower at the Lodge at Vail; and Chadwick's in Los Angeles. So we knew how to cook with bottarga and saba vinegar and make foie gras terrines—not how to cook for fifty people on four burners with a three-hundred-dollar budget! Because we did everything ourselves, we never had time to market our business, or even set up a Web site. We got all of our gigs through word of mouth and recommendations. Before we knew it, people were calling us those "food dudes," and the "underground caterers."

VINNY: People would call us the day before their party—for one hundred people—and we'd have to do all of the grocery shopping and prep in one day! Our food costs were out of this world, but we got a reputation as the two dudes who could pull anything off.

Jon: We've cooked for every event imaginable, from all-out celebrity bashes to backyard pig roasts and making grilled cheese sandwiches for a family dinner!

VINNY: Jonny gets a little overzealous sometimes. He'll say yes to practically anything, the crazier the better.

Jon: Admit it, you love it! The only job we say no to is cooking a romantic dinner for two; that's where we draw the line.

VINNY: In the beginning, we weren't even doing the cooking in a professional kitchen. We'd shop at the local supermarket, and then bring all of the provisions to our client's kitchen. It was like they had hired a personal chef for the day.

Jon: We had to approach menus with a different mindset than we did in the restaurant world. Because the budgets back then were always pretty bare-bones, we had to figure a way to feed the most people for the least money while still creating excellent and exciting food. It was as if our brains were two parts chef and one part homemaker! It was all about getting the most mileage out of certain ingredients, and making great food work within a very compressed time frame. Plus the food had to be awesome, because in L.A., word of mouth is everything.

VINNY: These days it's no longer just the two of us, a butane burner, and one pan, but we always remember the lessons we learned back then. Why use three pans (or more) when one will do? Why blow your entire food budget on loins of veal and exotic, out-of-season produce when the most crowd-pleasing dishes in our repertoire are riffs on taco night and pancake breakfasts? The recipes in this book are inspired by dishes we made during our early catering days when we depended on one or two key pans, our good ol' local grocery store, and a limited amount of time and space.

Jon: You don't need a tricked-out kitchen to make a nice meal. The idea is to keep cooking easy. That's why the premise of this book is that you only need one pan for each dish, based on a pretty modest collection of six or seven basic pieces (see page 17). A few may need an extra baking sheet or saucepan, but most can be done start to finish in a single bowl, pan, or skillet. Sometimes, we upgrade that dish with an accompaniment or variation that might require an additional saucepan or mixing bowl, but if all you have is a roasting pan or a skillet, there are a few dozen recipes you'll be able to cook straight off the bat.

VINNY: Our recipes are straightforward, and we offer lots of great time-saving suggestions, variations, and ingredient alternatives in case you can't find something in your market.

Jon: For the record, though, this isn't a book that is just about quick cooking. There are definitely ones meant for Sundays when you have a few hours to braise lamb shanks or short ribs.

VINNY: Just as there are recipes for a Tuesday night when you're totally starving and just need to eat—now!

Jon: Quick dishes like the seared scallops with shiitakes and spinach on page 110, a dish we used to make a lot and the one that inspired this book, requires you to have everything prepped out before you fire up your skillet. That's the case with a lot of quick dishes. They don't give you time to mess around once you start cooking.

VINNY: That's why I like the long-cooking dishes. Once you get them in the pot or pan and in the oven, they're generally pretty hands-off. Then I'm free to make dessert or read a book or just hang out.

Jon: Vin's such a bookworm.

VINNY: Yeah, when I get the time!

Jon: Actually, we really don't get a lot of free time. We work with a small kitchen crew: us, our main man Frank, and a few other prep cooks. We don't have the time or staff to do a lot of stuff that restaurant chefs do. Making stock is a technique that we've chosen to lay off of.

VINNY: Some chefs use chicken and veal stock the same way they use salt: all the time! We hardly use them at all. From a practical standpoint, we don't have the kitchen space, the refrigerator space, or the freezer space for stocks, so we find other ways to build flavor, like by pan-searing or using ingredients such as wine, beer, ketchup, tomato paste, Tabasco sauce, Dijon or grainy mustard, or Worcestershire sauce.

Jon: And you'll never catch us using canned chicken broth! We'd rather use water than canned broth. That stuff is gnarly.

VINNY: Another thing you might find surprising is that we don't use black pepper all that much. Black pepper adds heat, and sometimes it's nice to keep the flavor of fish, chicken, or even a salad pure. If you use pepper a lot, you desensitize your palate—just like what happens when you get used to a really spicy salsa, and then need something even spicier to perk up your tacos, you know? Of course there are a few dishes in this book that scream for pepper—our tuna au poivre and Frank's clam chowder, for example. They're classics and we respect the pepper in them.

Jon: There are a lot of classics in this book: roasted chicken, Bolognese sauce, osso buco, and lemon bars.

VINNY: These are the dishes that our clients ask us to cook the most. People really get into the whole comfort thing.

Jon: Comfort foods are the building blocks of cooking. If you can fry chicken, you can fry fish. If you can make pancakes, why not try crêpes? Learn your basics and go from there.

VINNY: This book is about cooking on a budget—a time budget, an equipment budget, as well as a food budget. It's about all the great dishes you can make even if the only pan you own is a single non-stick skillet.

Jon: Or the cast-iron pan you found at a tag sale, or a Dutch oven you got as a shower gift.

VINNY: This book is about not letting your environment or means dictate what you can do. It's about turning what seems limited into a whole mess of possibilities.

Jon: It's about cooking with four burners, a couple of pans, and food from your grocery store. We hope it ends up being a book that inspires you to fill it up with grease stains and tagged corners!

VINNY: So go wash your hands and get to it!

The Story of Two Dudes

Jon: We met in 1999 at the Art Institute of Fort Lauderdale, where we went to culinary school.

VINNY: Jonny and I shared a mutual laugh during orientation—I don't even remember what we were laughing at!

Jon: We got to talking and realized we had a lot in common: we were both from Florida, we both were into chicks, surfing, food. From then on, we were buds.

VINNY: Our dorm was being renovated, so we decided to get an apartment together. We've lived together ever since.

Jon: I had worked in food service throughout high school, doing everything from washing dishes to cooking on the line. Working at these real-deal greasy spoons and red-sauce joints gave me a little industry experience—enough to know that I wanted to spend my life cooking. It kept me out of trouble, too!

VINNY: I didn't have as much practical hands-on experience as Jonny, but I liked to read about the great chefs, like Escoffier and Shizuo Tsujii. From the beginning we just complemented one another.

Jon: I got an interview with Michelle Bernstein, the renowned Miami chef, who, at the time, was at the Strand in South Beach. Vinny came along with me, and when I was offered the job as Michelle's assistant, Vinny got hired on as her pastry chef Kevin Kopsick's assistant. It was like buy one, get one free!

VINNY: We worked really well together.

Michelle would make us compete against each other peeling vegetables or racing to prep a dish. She schooled us. Working with her was really amazing and changed the way we thought about food.

Jon: We went from cooking culinary school–style food that was one step up from cafeteria food to making these really conceptualized and beautiful dishes.

VINNY: We were young, though, and wanted to learn from as many people as possible, so we decided to move on.

Jon: Other chefs told us to split up, to go our separate ways, but we decided early on that we worked best as a team.

VINNY: We hopped around from place to place. And on our rare nights off, we'd go out and drop serious cash on dinner.

Jon: We were still underage, but we figured out that if we ordered the most expensive bottle on the menu, we'd get served, no questions asked. It worked every time.

VINNY: By eating and drinking big, we were having fun and educating our palates. We ate in the some of the best restaurants on the East Coast, from Miami to Philadelphia and New York City.

Jon: In 2001, we decided to move to New York, to get an apartment with another friend who was also a cook.

VINNY: But he bailed. We didn't have enough cash to rent an apartment in NYC on our own, so we decided to learn how to snowboard instead! We got jobs at Wildflower, the super-elegant restaurant at the Lodge at Vail in Colorado.

Jon: It was great—we'd cook all night and snowboard all day. Sometimes, on our day off, we'd throw some osso buco or short ribs in the oven to cook for a few hours. Then, when we came home starving after a long day on the mountain, we'd feast!

VINNY: But we missed surfing and warm weather, so we packed our stuff into a pickup truck and moved to California. We cooked our way across the country, taking our time making the trek. In exchange for a place to crash, we'd cook for our hosts—friends, or friends of friends. We literally had two pans and a couple of knives.

Jon: When we got to Los Angeles, we scored jobs at Govind Armstrong and Ben Ford's restaurant, Chadwick's. It was a really great place, but unfortunately it closed three short months after opening.

VINNY: We didn't know what to do at this point. Go to Europe and *stage* in France or Italy? Go to Napa and work at the French Laundry? We just hung low for a while, cooked for friends, and friends of friends, like we had done on our way out to California. Before we knew it, we were getting calls to cater parties.

Jon: That's when we started Carmelized Productions.

VINNY: It was hard but fun, and we learned a ton. We'd cater pancake parties, tapas parties, aphrodisiac parties! Finally, in the summer of 2005 we were able to lease a kitchen space adjacent to a music venue on Hollywood Boulevard. When there was a show, the space we rented became a restaurant called the Blue Palms Lounge, and we'd be in charge of creating menus for concertgoers. When there wasn't a show, we used the kitchen space as our catering headquarters.

Jon: That's when our food really started to evolve. Because we were cooking out of a constant space that never changed, we were able to focus on making relationships with farmers and the top seafood and meat purveyors. We started focusing on cooking with seasonal ingredients, organic when possible, local when available.

VINNY: About a year later, through some crazy twist of fate, we got asked to be on the Food Network's *Iron Chef* show pitted against Cat Cora! If you ever see "Battle: Eggplant" scheduled to air, check us out!

Jon: Soon after our big debut, we got in a row with our landlord and moved out of the space. We were back to cooking renegade-style—cooking from our own kitchen in a Los Feliz bungalow. It was wild. True to form, this is when everything started happening. Lots of consulting gigs, a constant flow of catering jobs, a book deal, and an opportunity to create a reality show for Food Network.

VINNY: These days we're focusing on expanding the business and our new restaurant, Animal.

Jon: We want to make our reality live up to our dreams. That, and to make really good food at the same time!

POTS and PANS: THE ESSENTIALS

When we were thinking of the different pots and pans to use in this book, we decided to focus on the truly essential pieces, the ones that no kitchen should be without. Now, we have sauciers (saucepans with rounded sides) and industrial hotel pans that we use for roasting twenty pounds of pork butt at a time, but for a home kitchen, you can really get away with just a few key items to start. These are the ones that we think are the most important.

The BIG BOWL

With one large bowl, you can make a variety of dishes, from salads to ceviches. We prefer metal to glass because we can bang it around on the counter and in the sink without worrying that it will break. Wood is fine for salads, but don't use it for ceviche because the bowl will get a fishy smell. A handle on the side of the bowl and rubber on the bottom to prevent the bowl from sliding around when whisking are nice features, but not absolutely vital. (Hang on to the bowl with your hand and place a dampened paper towel or hand towel beneath the bowl and you'll accomplish the same thing.) Mixing bowls are one of the few pieces of equipment that you can cheap out on. Save your money for a good-quality skillet, roasting pan, or Dutch oven instead.

NONSTICK SKILLET

A nonstick skillet is only as good as its nonstick coating, and even if you take the best care of your pan, chances are that the nonstick coating will start flaking after a few years of use. Instead of making a big investment in an expensive nonstick skillet, buy an inexpensive one that has moderate heft and a comfortable, welded-on handle (the screwed-on handles can come loose and get wobbly with time). You really shouldn't spend more than fifty bucks on a nonstick skillet. A twelve-inch nonstick can fry a frittata just as well as it can accommodate long fish fillets. It's the size we recommend to start with, though a small eight-inch nonstick comes in handy for frying eggs.

CLASSIC SKILLET

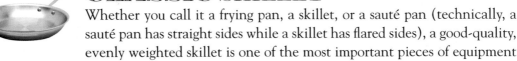

Whether you call it a frying pan, a skillet, or a sauté pan (technically, a sauté pan has straight sides while a skillet has flared sides), a good-quality, evenly weighted skillet is one of the most important pieces of equipment in your kitchen. This is the pan you'll turn to time and time again for searing meats, sautéing vegetables, and making pan sauces. The handle should be oven-safe so the pan can go from the stovetop to the oven or broiler without a problem. Searing meat without scorching the browned bits on the bottom of the pan is really important, making a heavy-gauge steel-clad aluminum- or copper-core skillet your best option. Enameled cast iron works well, too, but we find it on the heavy side. If you want to work on your biceps while you cook, though, go for it! As with the nonstick skillet, a twelve-inch skillet is the size to start with.

DUTCH Oven

This is a piece of equipment worth investing in. It's used for slow, wet cooking methods, such as braising short ribs in beer or slow-cooking lamb shanks with wine. Since it's constructed for stovetop-to-oven cooking, a Dutch oven is usually made of heavier material that can withstand long stays in a hot oven. Even though most recipes that call for a Dutch oven can technically be made in a soup pot, the difference is that the heat will be distributed more evenly in the heavier-gauge Dutch oven, which definitely comes in handy when browning meat and vegetables. A good Dutch oven should have a tight-fitting lid that will retain steam, and both pot and lid should be oven-safe (watch out for flimsy plastic knobs on the top of lids). A six-quart Dutch oven can comfortably hold big pieces of meat and roasts and is deep enough to contain any liquid you add for the cooking process. In a pinch you can make soup, boil water for pasta, and deep-fry in a Dutch oven, making it a really valuable all-around player in the kitchen.

ROASTING PAN

When you're dry roasting without much liquid, this is the pan to choose. It should be large and deep enough to hold a six-bone prime rib or a Thanksgiving turkey, with handles that are easy to get a good, solid grip on. Though we don't include any recipes in this book for making gravy or pan sauces in a roasting pan (to do that you'd remove the meat, place the roasting pan on your stovetop over medium-high heat, deglaze the pan with liquid such as stock or wine, and then add butter or cream to make a sauce), we do sometimes roast vegetables along with a protein (as in the Cuban-Style Roast Pork on page 196 or the Sherried Salmon with Cipollini Onions on page 186). Both are reasons to invest in a roasting pan with a thick, even, and heavy-gauge bottom. If you can't devote that kind of money to a pan, then you can always place a baking sheet (see page 21) underneath a flimsier roasting pan to provide a little more support. Be sure to purchase a roasting rack along with your roasting pan if it doesn't come with one. These are handy for elevating chickens or pork loins to circulate air for more even browning.

In a pinch, a half-sheet pan (see page 21) can be a perfectly serviceable stand-in for a roasting pan, though its shorter sides won't contain as much liquid or other ingre-

dients as the higher-sided roasting pan will. But if you're stuck, many of these recipes will work with a good heavy-guage sheet pan, a good reason to add one of these to your short list.

BAKING DISH

We use a 9 by 13-inch 3-quart glass baking dish for all of our desserts. You could get all fancy here if you wanted and buy a pricey glazed porcelain or clayware baking dish, but we opt for the tried and true (and cheap) glass Pyrex dish for a few reasons. One, it's cool to peek into the oven and see right through the baking dish to check the color of what's baking (which is why we also prefer glass over metal baking pans). Two, its curved corners are easy to clean. Three, if it breaks, it's no problem. Go to any department store or even a grocery store and you can replace it for less than fifteen dollars.

Eventually, if you really get into baking, you'll want to load up on springform pans, fluted tart pans, and muffin tins—just for starters. But for now, you'll be shocked and awed at how many great desserts you can turn out using just this one pan. Check; you've probably got one in the cabinet somewhere already!

SAUCEPAN

We didn't include a saucepan chapter in this book because you can't really make a meal in a saucepan. That said, a saucepan is useful for lots of things, such as making rice, polenta, fruit compotes and sauces, and cream sauces (crème anglaise, béarnaise, and more); heating stock; and blanching small-cut vegetables. Saucepans have straight edges and sharp corners while *sauciers* have rounded corners; they're fairly interchangeable, though sauciers are a little better for making cream sauces because you can really get into the corners. We tend to prefer good-quality heavy-gauge steel-clad aluminum- or copper-core saucepans because they heat evenly and retain heat—qualities that are vital for rice and cream sauces. We like long handles to keep our hands away from the heat, and we prefer welded handles or riveted ones to those attached to the base by screws that can come loose with time. A good 2- or 3-quart saucepan should last awhile. Oh, and here's a cool tip: if you can't find your saucepan's lid, use a large metal bowl set into the saucepan instead. Just make sure the bottom of the bowl is at least a couple of inches from what's inside, and use a pot holder to lift it off—it gets hot!

BEYOND *the* BASICS

None of the pots below is essential to our recipes, but the more you start cooking, the more uses you'll find for these second-tier favorites. Throughout this book you'll see notations indicating where they can be substituted for the pan called for.

SOUP Pot

You can do almost anything in a soup pot. Boil pasta, steam mussels, fry chicken, sauté vegetables, make mashed potatoes—you could even use it as a mixing bowl if you wanted to! What's important in a soup pot is that it be deep enough to hold a lot of liquid and that it have a thick bottom so you can brown meats and vegetables evenly before adding liquid and deglazing the pot (all those little browned bits add tons of flavor to soups and stews).

CAST-IRON SKILLET

You can buy a new cast-iron skillet or pick one up at a yard sale. If used pans skeeve you out, then buy the new one. If a pan with a little bit of history and wear appeals to you, go for the used model. Unlike other pots and pans, cast-iron equipment gets better as it ages, and the more broken in a cast-iron pan is, the better the natural nonstick coating (achieved through years of frying chicken and bacon!). Check out page 83 for more about cast-iron skillets.

BAKING SHEET *or* Half-Sheet PAN

Though baking sheets are pretty standard in most kitchens, we didn't give them their own chapter because so many items that can be cooked on a baking sheet can easily work in a more versatile roasting pan, too. Baking sheets are definitely the way to go, though, for baking cookies, toasting bread, and lining an oven rack to catch drips from a roasting pan or skillet. A lot of people like nonstick or insulated baking sheets, but go into any pro kitchen and you'll find a durable aluminum-coated steel half- or full-sized rimmed sheet pan. This is the kind we use. It's made from heavy-gauge metal so food cooks evenly and it doesn't warp. Line it with parchment paper or a silicone mat, or grease it with pan spray or butter, and it works even better than nonstick. A rimmed edge is critical so food doesn't fall off the sides when you go to stir or turn it. Before buying, be sure to measure the size of your oven. Half-sheets work well in most ovens, but if you have a pullout broiler drawer rather than a broiler element in the oven, you may have to buy a smaller baking sheet.

GIVENS

We're assuming you already have these in your kitchen; if not, get yourself to a kitchenware store or a chef supply house and stock up before you start cooking.

Chef's Knife or Santoku Knife

Hold it in your hand to test the weight and the fit of the handle before buying. A chef's knife (also called a French knife) has a tapered blade that rocks as you chop, while a Japanese santoku knife has a more straight-edged blade with channels on one side of the blade to prevent food from sticking to it.

Paring Knife

Short and sweet, this is our cutlery of choice for hulling strawberries, slicing gashes into fish, and peeking into the center of a cooked steak to check its doneness. You can go cheap or expensive here. When a cheap paring knife goes dull, it probably costs about the same amount to replace it as it does to sharpen it. Because you're not handling the knife in the same way as you would a chef's knife, the construction quality of a paring knife is less important than it is for a chef's knife.

Digital Thermometer

You can get a stab-and-jab instant-read model or one of those digital contraptions with a probe connected by a heat-proof wire to a timer and an alarm that goes off when your chicken or roast reaches the desired temperature.

Colander

For straining and draining.

Silicone Spatula

Essential for cooking in nonstick pans, and also useful for stirring risottos, deglazing pans, scraping batters into baking dishes, and much more. Silicone, unlike regular rubber, won't melt in hot liquids. Get the kind with a bowled scraper (called a spoonula); it can be use to scoop ingredients onto plates for serving.

Whisk

For making dressings, pan sauces, even guacamole and mashed potatoes. Choose a sturdy, medium-sized metal one.

Tongs

Keep tongs basic: all you need is long metal tongs that are easy to grip and grab. Make sure they're long enough to stick into a pot while keeping your hands safely out of it! Tongs also come in handy for grabbing hot pot lids, pulling out a hot oven rack, or reaching that bottle of good alcohol you've hidden in the back of the cabinet.

Measuring Spoons and Cups
Plastic, metal, whatever. The oblong spoons are nice because they fit into narrow-necked spice jars. For measuring liquids, we like plastic measuring cups since they're fairly indestructible.

Mixing Bowls
We prefer metal to glass or ceramic. They're goof proof and safer in the kitchen. Every kitchen should have at least two (one medium, one large); a graduated set of four or five is better still, and can be had for about twenty-five bucks.

THE BIG
BOWL

Jon: We live in California, and in California, the number-one most popular dish here is a salad! Well, after burgers. And tacos . . .

VINNY: Salads are one of my all-time favorite things. The combinations—even just for salad dressings—are endless.

Jon: Our favorite salads are composed salads that give you multiple flavors and textures in each bite.

VINNY: You want to mix crunchy with tender, salty with sweet, and tangy with tart or bitter. Like escarole with apples, Parmigiano-Reggiano, and walnuts.

Jon: In the winter we might use pomegranate seeds or shaved fennel. In the summer we'll go with stuff from the farmer's market, like wild arugula or lamb's quarters, a tender green similar to purslane.

VINNY: I get a lot of inspiration by going to the Santa Monica farmer's market. It's just amazing.

Jon: I know when Vin has been to the farmer's market because our fridge is packed with like a flat of amazing strawberries or some totally obscure and random baby green no one has ever heard of before! Most often, these ingredients are destined for the salad bowl.

VINNY: Even if they don't get used for a salad, we use the mixing bowl for other no-cook, stir-and-serve dishes like guacamole and ceviche.

Jon: You can even serve these dishes straight from the mixing bowl.

VINNY: Whether destined for a salad or a dip, we always wash produce as soon as we get home from the market and before we put them away in the fridge.

Jon: Washing everything ahead of time makes tossing a salad together easier, too. All of your ingredients are good to go straight from the fridge.

VINNY: I have a hangup about putting dirty vegetables in the fridge. You don't want to cross-contaminate other clean items you might have in there with the dirt and other stuff they may have on them. Make cleaning everything a part of putting your groceries away. Wash them up, then place them in a plastic container lined with paper towels to absorb any extra moisture.

Jon: If your washed greens need perking up, place them in a big bowl of ice water for a minute. There's nothing better than cold, crisp lettuce.

VINNY: A final word of advice: always taste your salad as you go. Sometimes the difference between a good salad and a great one is a squeeze of acid or a little salt.

MENU

Peaches *and* **Arugula** *with*
ALMONDS,
RADISHES, *and* PARM

Winter Fennel Salad *with*
CINNAMON VINAIGRETTE

WATERMELON *and*
Mizuna Salad *with* FETA

THE **Greek**

Creamy TARRAGON-**Dressed**
BUTTER LETTUCE, *Smashed*
Croutons, *and* GRANA

Carrots, DANDELION GREENS,
and **Cumin-Raisin**
VINAIGRETTE

DRESSINGS FOR THE ARCHIVES:
• Real Caesar • Classic French • Warm Bacon
Vinaigrette • Creamy Blue Cheese • Miso-Honey
• Green Goddess • Roasted Garlic Ranch
• Our Basic Vinaigrette

Our GUAC

HAWAIIAN Poke

Peruvian-Style
CITRUS CEVICHE

A Few Words on Oil

Unless we specifically want the briny, full flavor of a good virgin olive oil, we often make our own blended oil with 80 percent grapeseed oil and 20 percent extra-virgin olive oil. We find this combo gives us a nice mellow and clean flavor with just a hint of olive, and it's a whole lot more economical, too. It's great for salad dressings and in other dishes where you don't necessarily want the boldness of olive oil. Since virgin oil is so heat-sensitive, we usually prefer to use straight-up olive oil (not extra-virgin) whenever subjecting the fat to a flame.

We like grapeseed oil because of its pure flavor and incredibly high smoking point, which means you can heat it to very high temperatures without burning it. Canola oil works well, too. But we're really not into vegetable oil; you just don't know which oils were blended to make it, and we prefer to have as much control over the flavor of our food as possible. Try mixing up a batch of your own and see for yourself. At the very least, you will have stretched that bottle of pricey extra-virgin.

Peaches *and* **Arugula** *with* ALMONDS, RADISHES, *and* PARM

VINNY: This salad reminds me of why I got infatuated with salads in the first place. It's the ultimate in composed salads, bringing together all kinds of salty, sweet, bitter, juicy, dry, and crunchy characteristics. Watercress works here, too, if you prefer it to arugula.

Jon: Peppery arugula provides a nice contrast to peaches, but you can use other stone fruits here, too, such as nectarines or even apricots. Grill the peaches for a great charred flavor, or add paper-thin slices of prosciutto or crispy fried speck for a main-course salad.

WHISK the oils, lemon juice, and sugar in a large bowl. Add the peaches and toss gently to combine. Gently mix in the arugula and salt. Transfer to a serving bowl or to individual plates and top with the almonds, radishes, and cheese. Serve immediately.

SERVES **6**

2 tablespoons grapeseed or canola oil

1½ teaspoons extra-virgin olive oil

Juice of 2 lemons

1½ teaspoons sugar

3 ripe peaches, pitted and thinly sliced

4 cups arugula

2 teaspoons kosher salt

¼ cup toasted whole almonds (see Note)

3 radishes, sliced paper-thin

1 2-ounce chunk Parmigiano-Reggiano cheese, shaved with a vegetable peeler

---

toasting nuts and seeds

The most reliable method is to heat your oven to 400°F, place the nuts on a rimmed sheet pan, and toast them until they're fragrant and lightly browned, 5 to 10 minutes depending on the type of nut (slivered almonds and peanuts take less time; whole almonds, walnuts, and pecans require more). Shake the pan midway through toasting so the nuts brown evenly. Smaller nuts and seeds, such as pistachios, sliced almonds, pine nuts, pumpkin seeds, and sesame seeds, can be toasted in a dry skillet on your stovetop over medium-high heat. Shake the pan often to prevent them from burning, and transfer the nuts or seeds to a small bowl as soon as they're toasted since they can burn from the carryover heat in the skillet even after you turn off the heat.

WINTER FENNEL SALAD
with Cinnamon VINAIGRETTE

FOR THE SALAD

4 baby fennel bulbs or
   2 medium fennel bulbs
2 apples (try Pink Lady or
   Braeburn), cored and
   halved
½ lemon (optional)
½ cup halved grapes (we like
   Red Flame or Muscat)
3 tablespoons toasted pine
   nuts (see Note, page 29)
2 teaspoons finely chopped
   fresh chives
1 teaspoon kosher salt
1 2-ounce chunk Pecorino
   cheese, shaved with a
   vegetable peeler

FOR THE VINAIGRETTE

2 tablespoons champagne
   vinegar
1 teaspoon pure maple syrup
   (preferably grade A)
¼ teaspoon ground cinnamon
½ teaspoon kosher salt
1 shallot, peeled, halved
   lengthwise, and thinly
   sliced lengthwise
3 tablespoons canola or
   grapeseed oil
2 tablespoons extra-virgin
   olive oil

Jon: The texture and unique licorice-y flavor of fennel rocks out with apples and cinnamon. Fennel and apples are so versatile. You wouldn't think that they would work together, but they do. Also, watch out when you toast those pine nuts . . .

VINNY: Yeah, when we competed against Cat Cora on *Iron Chef,* we totally burnt them—multiple times—because we kept getting distracted. It's best to toast them low and slow, in a skillet over low heat. Shake the pan a lot to encourage even browning. This way, you brown the nuts all the way through without scorching them like we did!

HALVE and core the fennel bulbs and trim off the stalks. Chop 1 tablespoon of the fronds to garnish the salads; discard the rest. Slice the fennel bulbs and apples very thin and cut into matchsticks. If you are making the salad more than 10 minutes ahead of time, squeeze the lemon over them to prevent them from browning, and set aside.

Whisk the champagne vinegar, maple syrup, cinnamon, and salt together in a large bowl. Add the shallots and drizzle in the oils while whisking to incorporate.

Add the fennel, apples, grapes, pine nuts, chives, and salt to the vinaigrette and toss to combine. Transfer to a serving bowl or to individual plates, top with the cheese, garnish with the reserved fennel fronds, and serve.

SERVES 6

Watermelon *and* MIZUNA SALAD *with* Feta

VINNY: Make this for your friends and they'll think you're on your game. Even though feta and watermelon is a classic combo, the sweet-salty pairing is just unusual enough to really impress people. That said, if you're not into the sweet and salty thing, you could do this with chopped ripe tomatoes instead of the watermelon and it would still be great.

Jon: For a more substantial salad, poach some peeled and deveined shrimp (four or five medium shrimp per person) in a saucepan with water, some lemon juice, a bay leaf, a few black peppercons, a spring of thyme, and a little sea salt until the shrimp are just opaque, about 2½ minutes.

PLACE the watermelon, all but 2 tablespoons of the feta, the mint, basil, lemon juice, oils, and salt in a large bowl and gently toss together. Let the mixture stand for 1 minute, then add the mizuna or arugula and toss to coat. Transfer to a serving bowl or to individual plates, sprinkle with the reserved 2 tablespoons of feta, and serve.

SERVES 6

3 cups seedless watermelon cubes

¾ cup (about 4 ounces) crumbled feta cheese

8 fresh mint leaves, stacked and roughly chopped

6 fresh basil leaves, stacked and roughly chopped

Juice of 2 lemons

1 tablespoon extra-virgin olive oil

1 tablespoon grapeseed or canola oil

2 teaspoons kosher salt

2 cups mizuna or arugula

---

how to cut a watermelon

For a small round watermelon, slice off the ends so it stands upright, then slice lengthwise down the melon to trim off the rind (as you would an orange). You'll be left with a cube that you can then chop or dice as you like. For a big zeppelin-shaped melon, cut it in half widthwise, trim off the rounded ends, stand it upright, and trim off the rind lengthwise. Then cut up the cube however you like. If the small or large watermelon has seeds, slice the trimmed cube lengthwise into four quarters and slice away the seedbed, then cut up as you like.

The GREEK

FOR THE DRESSING

2 tablespoons red wine vinegar

6 pitted kalamata olives, very finely chopped (almost to a paste)

2 teaspoons finely chopped fresh marjoram

1 teaspoon finely chopped fresh thyme

½ teaspoon sugar

¼ teaspoon kosher salt

2 tablespoons extra-virgin olive oil

2 tablespoons canola or grapeseed oil

FOR THE SALAD

4 cups thinly sliced escarole (from one 1–1½-pound head)

½ English (seedless) cucumber, peeled and thinly sliced, or 1 medium cucumber, halved, seeds removed using a teaspoon, and thinly sliced

½ cup whole grape tomatoes or halved cherry tomatoes

½ recipe Crunchy Fried Feta (page 65) or ½ cup crumbled feta cheese

¼ cup Pickled Red Onions (recipe follows)

½ teaspoon kosher salt

Jon: This salad reminds me of my boy Lou, who helps us out on the line once in a while when we're scheduled to cook a monster party. Lou's grandparents are from Greece, and he's always talking about the food they cooked for him while he was growing up.

VINNY: That said, I really like French feta better than Greek—it's nice and creamy and fries up beautifully. Sorry, Lou!

WHISK the vinegar with the olives, marjoram, thyme, sugar, and salt in a large bowl. Drizzle in the oils while whisking to incorporate. Add the escarole, cucumbers, and tomatoes and toss to coat.

Transfer to a platter or individual plates and top with the feta and pickled onions, sprinkle with the salt, and serve.

SERVES 4 TO 6

+1 pan: pickled red onions

Pickling is a great way to get another five days out of your red onions once they start to get a little soft. We use these pickled onions all over the place: in salads, on burgers, for tacos. Once you run out, save the liquid and reuse it for your next batch. You can even use the liquid in place of vinegar in salad dressings or to add an edge to a sauce.

Place 1 thinly sliced red onion in a medium, heatproof bowl. Bring ½ cup red wine vinegar and ½ cup sugar to a simmer in a small nonreactive saucepan and cook until the sugar is dissolved. Pour the mixture over the onions and set aside until cool, then refrigerate in an airtight plastic container for up to 2 weeks.

MAKES 1 CUP OF PICKLED RED ONIONS

Creamy Tarragon-DRESSED BUTTER Lettuce, Smashed CROUTONS, and GRANA

Jon: I feel like I'm always hunting down the croutons in a salad. In this one, we smash them up so you get a little bit of crouton in every bite. It's a bit rustic in a texturally cool kind of way.

VINNY: Butter lettuces, such as Boston and Bibb, stand up really nicely to a creamy dressing, but if you can't find them in your market, iceberg is our second runner-up.

PLACE the croutons in a resealable plastic bag (make sure that there isn't any trapped air in the bag) and, using the bottom of your mixing bowl, press down on the croutons to smash them into uneven bits. Set aside.

In a large bowl, whisk together the mayo, sour cream, lemon juice, tarragon, chives, salt, and pepper. Add 1 to 2 tablespoons water, just enough to thin the dressing to a medium-bodied consistency, like that of a creamy ranch dressing

Place the greens in the bowl and toss gently with your hands to coat with the dressing. Transfer to a serving bowl or individual plates, top with the cheese and smashed croutons, and serve.

SERVES 4

+1 pan: homemade croutons

Heat your oven to 300°F. Place ¼ cup extra-virgin olive oil and 1½ teaspoons kosher salt in a large bowl. Add 6 cups of ½-inch bread cubes (about 1 French baguette) and toss to combine. Transfer the cubes to a rimmed sheet pan and toast until the cubes are just starting to color and get crispy, about 25 minutes, stirring the croutons midway through baking. Set aside to cool, and use immediately or store in a plastic bag for up to 1 week.

---

1 cup homemade croutons (see below) or store-bought croutons

FOR THE TARRAGON VINAIGRETTE

3 tablespoons mayonnaise
3 tablespoons sour cream
Juice of ½ lemon
2 teaspoons finely chopped fresh tarragon, a few leaves reserved for garnish
1 teaspoon finely chopped fresh chives, a pinch reserved for garnish
1 teaspoon kosher salt
1 teaspoon freshly ground black pepper

FOR THE SALAD

2 heads of Bibb or Boston lettuce, quartered
1 4-ounce chunk Grana Padana or Parmigiano-Reggiano cheese, shaved with a vegetable peeler

CARROTS, Dandelion Greens, *and* CUMIN-RAISIN VINAIGRETTE

¼ cup plus 2 tablespoons
  sherry vinegar

¼ cup golden raisins

1 shallot, peeled, halved
  lengthwise, and thinly
  sliced

2 teaspoons ground cumin

1 teaspoon finely chopped
  fresh thyme

2 teaspoons kosher salt

1 teaspoon sugar

2 tablespoons canola or
  grapeseed oil

2 tablespoons extra-virgin
  olive oil

4 medium carrots, peeled,
  then shaved into fine
  strips with the peeler or
  very thinly sliced

2 cups dandelion greens
  (about 1 bunch), stripped
  from stems

VINNY: This is our California take on a popular beet salad created by chef Mark Militello, for whom we worked when we were just starting out. A customer favorite, it's probably still served at at least one of his restaurants in Florida.

Jon: Baby carrots are so sweet and tender, you can't even begin to compare them to machine-trimmed bagged "baby" carrots that supermarkets sell. If there aren't any true baby carrots in your market, medium carrots will do.

MICROWAVE the ¼ cup of sherry vinegar in a microwaveable bowl in 30-second increments until it is hot. Add the raisins, cover with plastic wrap, and steep until the raisins are plump and have completely absorbed the vinegar, about 5 minutes.

Pour the remaining 2 tablespoons of sherry vinegar into a large bowl and whisk with the shallots, cumin, thyme, salt, and sugar. Whisk in the oils and then add the raisins. Add the carrots and the dandelion greens and toss gently to coat. Transfer to a platter and serve.

SERVES 4 TO 6

---

note

This recipe works well as a roasted side dish, too. Preheat your oven to 450°F. Instead of shaving the carrots, slice them into ¼- to ½-inch planks, drizzle a little olive oil over them, sprinkle with salt, and then place them on a greased baking sheet. Roast until tender and then proceed with the recipe above.

Dressings for the Archives

We're obsessed with dressing made from scratch. It's so easy to make, and it delivers such amazing results. These dressings are like classic rock: familiar, comforting, always satisfying. Each makes enough to dress 8 to 10 cups of greens; however, that said, don't limit them to the salad bowl. Dressings make great sauces for a seared duck breast, chicken wings, or a sandwich. They're excellent with raw veggies for a snack or a party app; or toss them with steamed or sautéed vegetables for a quick side dish.

REAL CAESAR

WHISK the egg yolk with the garlic, anchovy, shallot, Worcestershire, lemon juice, Tabasco, mustard, salt, and pepper in a large bowl. While whisking, drizzle in three quarters of the oil, and then whisk in the vinegar and the cheese. Taste the dressing and add more oil if you prefer a thinner Caesar dressing. Refrigerate until serving (this dressing must be used the same day that it is made).

NOTE If you have health concerns about using a raw egg, you can omit it.

MAKES A GENEROUS ¾ CUP FOR 8 CUPS OF GREENS

1 large egg yolk (see Note)
2 garlic cloves, minced
1 anchovy fillet, minced
1½ teaspoons minced shallot
1½ teaspoons Worcestershire sauce
1 teaspoon fresh lemon juice
¾ teaspoon Tabasco sauce
½ teaspoon Dijon mustard
1 teaspoon kosher salt
½ teaspoon freshly ground black pepper
½ cup plus 1½ tablespoons grapeseed oil
2 tablespoons red wine vinegar
½ cup finely grated Parmigiano-Reggiano cheese

CLASSIC FRENCH

WHISK the egg yolk with the ketchup, garlic, mustard, sugar, chives, and salt in a large bowl. While whisking, slowly drizzle in three quarters of the oil, and then whisk in the vinegar. Taste and add more oil if you prefer a thinner French dressing. Refrigerate until serving (this dressing must be used the same day that it is made).

NOTE If you have health concerns about using a raw egg, you can omit it.

MAKES 1½ CUPS FOR 8 TO 10 CUPS OF GREENS

1 large egg yolk (see Note)
½ cup ketchup
3 garlic cloves, very finely chopped
1½ teaspoons Dijon mustard
2 tablespoons sugar
1 tablespoon finely chopped fresh chives
1 teaspoon kosher salt
½ cup canola or grapeseed oil
⅓ cup white vinegar

WARM BACON VINAIGRETTE

4 slices bacon

¼ small red onion, finely chopped

3 tablespoons red wine vinegar or sherry vinegar

3 tablespoons canola or grapeseed oil

1 tablespoon finely chopped fennel bulb or fresh tarragon (optional)

1 teaspoon sugar

1 teaspoon kosher salt

¾ teaspoon grainy mustard

HEAT a medium skillet over high heat for 1 minute. Add the bacon and reduce the heat to medium. Cook the bacon until browned and crispy on both sides, about 8 minutes total. Drain the bacon on a paper-towel-lined plate. Once it is cool, crumble the bacon.

Place 1 tablespoon of the warm bacon fat (reheat if necessary) in a large bowl. Whisk in the remaining ingredients and add the crumbled bacon just before serving.

MAKES ⅔ CUP FOR 8 CUPS OF GREENS

CREAMY BLUE CHEESE

⅓ cup crumbled blue cheese (preferably Maytag blue cheese)

¼ cup mayonnaise

¼ cup sour cream

3 garlic cloves, very finely chopped

1 tablespoon finely chopped fresh flat-leaf parsley

1½ teaspoons finely chopped fresh chives

½ small shallot, finely chopped

1 teaspoon kosher salt

2 teaspoons freshly ground black pepper

¼ cup buttermilk

2 tablespoons white vinegar

MIX the blue cheese, mayonnaise, and sour cream together in a large bowl. Stir in the garlic, parsley, chives, shallots, salt, and pepper. Mix the buttermilk and vinegar together in a liquid measuring cup and, while whisking, stir the liquid into the blue cheese mixture.

Refrigerate until serving or up to 2 days (the dressing will get more oniony the longer it is held in the fridge.)

MAKES 1⅓ CUPS FOR 8 TO 10 CUPS OF GREENS

MISO-HONEY

WHISK the rice vinegar, honey, miso, and soy sauce in a medium bowl. Whisk in the oil and refrigerate until serving, or up to 1 week.

MAKES 1¼ CUPS FOR 8 TO 10 CUPS OF GREENS

⅓ cup unseasoned rice vinegar

⅓ cup honey

4 tablespoons miso (brown, red, or white)

1 tablespoon soy sauce

⅓ cup canola or grapeseed oil

GREEN GODDESS

PLACE all of the ingredients in a blender jar in the order listed and purée until smooth, scraping down the blender as necessary. Refrigerate until serving or up to 5 days.

MAKES 1½ CUPS FOR 8 TO 10 CUPS OF GREENS

⅓ cup champagne or white wine vinegar

⅓ cup mayonnaise

⅓ cup sour cream

2 teaspoons fresh lemon juice

3 garlic cloves, roughly chopped

½ cup finely chopped fresh flat-leaf parsley

3 tablespoons finely chopped fresh chives

1½ teaspoons finely chopped shallot

1½ teaspoons finely chopped fresh tarragon

2 anchovy fillets

⅓ cup sesame tahini

ROASTED GARLIC RANCH

1 head of garlic

⅓ cup mayonnaise

⅓ cup sour cream

⅓ cup buttermilk

1 tablespoon red wine
vinegar

2 tablespoons finely chopped
fresh chives

1½ teaspoons kosher salt

1½ teaspoons finely ground
black pepper

1 tablespoon fresh lemon
juice

PREHEAT your oven to 375°F. Slice off the top fourth of the head of garlic so all of the cloves are exposed. Wrap the head in aluminum foil and roast until the garlic is tender, 30 to 45 minutes. Remove from the oven and set aside to cool.

Squeeze the garlic from the base of the head into a large bowl. Whisk to break up and then whisk in the mayonnaise and sour cream. Mix in the buttermilk followed by the red wine vinegar, chives, salt, and pepper. Whisk in the lemon juice and refrigerate until serving, or up to 5 days.

MAKES 1½ CUPS FOR 8 TO 10 CUPS OF GREENS

OUR BASIC VINAIGRETTE

⅓ cup vinegar (such as
balsamic, champagne, red
wine, sherry, or
white wine)

1 teaspoon Dijon mustard

1 tablespoon finely chopped
shallot or fresh chives

1½ teaspoons finely chopped
fresh herbs (such as basil,
chervil, marjoram, oregano,
tarragon, or thyme)

2 teaspoons sugar (omit
if you're using a sweet
vinegar, such as balsamic)

1 teaspoon kosher salt

⅓ cup oil (such as canola,
grapeseed, or extra-virgin
olive)

IN a large bowl whisk together the vinegar, mustard, shallots or chives, herbs, sugar (if using), and salt. While whisking, slowly drizzle in the oil. Refrigerate until serving or up to 1 week (some herbs, such as basil, will darken as they sit in the fridge). Shake vigorously to reemulsify before serving.

MAKES ¾ CUP FOR 8 CUPS OF GREENS

OUR Guac

Jon: People go nuts for great guacamole. Our secret is a little sour cream. It makes the guac nice and creamy, and the lactic acid prevents the avocados from browning, at least for a couple of hours. If you don't do dairy, just leave out the sour cream.

VINNY: What is key is to have soft and buttery avocados, ideally ripe enough to mash with a whisk. You're in for a world of hurt if your avocados are too hard.

HALVE and pit the avocados, then scoop them out of their skins and into a large bowl. Using a fork, smash the avocados until they're semi-smooth and still a little lumpy. Add the remaining ingredients and mix gently to combine. Taste for seasoning, and serve immediately or cover tightly with plastic wrap and refrigerate for 2 hours maximum.

SERVES 8 TO 10

4 Hass avocados

¼ cup sour cream

2 or 3 jalapeños (depending on how spicy you like your guac), seeded, deveined, and finely diced

2 small plum tomatoes, halved, seeded, and finely diced (about ¼ cup)

Juice of 1½ limes (about 3 tablespoons)

1 tablespoon extra-virgin olive oil

1 garlic clove, finely chopped

¼ cup finely chopped fresh cilantro

1½ teaspoons kosher salt

HAWAIIAN Poke

½ cup mirin

⅓ cup soy sauce

¼ small sweet onion, such as
Maui or Vidalia, finely
chopped

1 scallion, white and green
parts, thinly sliced on
the bias

1 tablespoon sambal
(or to taste)

1 pound best-quality tuna,
cut into ½-inch cubes

2 teaspoons toasted sesame
seeds (see page 29)

tip
For a quick party dish,
make poke and serve it in
warmed corn tortillas as a
twist on fish tacos. To warm
tortillas, heat them for
about 10 seconds on each
side in a dry skillet over
medium heat until warmed
and pliable. Or microwave
them by stacking the
tortillas on a plate with
damp paper towels sepa-
rating the tortillas. Place a
damp paper towel on top
and microwave in 20-
second increments until
warmed through.

JON: Poke, a Hawaiian raw fish salad pronounced po-kay,
reminds me of fun days spearfishing on the island when
you know the rest of your crew is back in L.A. working! We
were inspired to create this spicy take on poke after trying
a similar version in Hawaii at the Poke Man's place in
Honolulu. It was so good I scarfed it down in minutes.

VINNY: Since you'll be eating this raw, it's important
to buy the best-quality and freshest tuna you can get. Look
for tuna that's deep purple with very little or no white in it.
The white part is sinewy, and since this is a raw dish, it's
not going to break down during cooking. If you can't find
sambal chile paste, you can use sriracha or Tabasco sauce
instead. This is one of the few dishes we like to make on
the spicy side.

WHISK the mirin, soy sauce, onion, scallion, and sambal in a
large bowl. Add the tuna and mix gently with your hands to
coat. Cover with plastic wrap and marinate in the refrigerator for 1 to 2 hours.

Transfer the fish to a serving bowl or to individual bowls,
discarding the marinade, and sprinkle with the sesame seeds
before serving.

SERVES 4 TO 6

PERUVIAN-Style CITRUS CEVICHE

Jon: When we worked at the Strand in Miami, Manny the dishwasher, a Peruvian guy, used to make the most amazing ceviche. The acid in the citrus juice pseudo-cooks the fish and makes it opaque. Because it's "cooked" by the acid, a lot of people who don't do tartare, sashimi, or poke like ceviche.

VINNY: This is so simple and easy. You can make it up to one day ahead of serving, but the longer the fish sits, the firmer it gets because of the acid. I like it after an hour or two of marinating, while the fish is still tender. In Peru the ceviche gets sided with Peruvian corn nuts or even popcorn, but it's delicious without, too.

WHISK the lemon, lime, and orange juices together in a large bowl. Add the jalapeño, bell peppers, cilantro, sugar, and salt and whisk to combine. Add the fish and toss gently with your hands. Cover the bowl with plastic wrap and marinate in the refrigerator for 1 to 2 hours. Serve in bowls with popcorn or corn nuts on the side.

SERVES 4 TO 6

¼ cup fresh lemon juice (from about 1 lemon)

¼ cup fresh lime juice (from about 2 limes)

¼ cup fresh orange juice (from about ½ orange)

1 jalapeño or serrano chile (seeded and deveined for less heat), finely diced

1 tablespoon finely diced red bell pepper

1 tablespoon finely diced yellow bell pepper

1 tablespoon chopped fresh cilantro

2 teaspoons sugar

1½ teaspoons kosher salt

2 8-ounce skinless fluke, grouper, or halibut fillets, cut into ¾-inch cubes

Popcorn or corn nuts, for serving (optional)

NONSTICK
SKILLET

VINNY: This is the skillet that we carried with us on the road when we traveled cross-country from Florida to Los Angeles.

Jon: It was great because, since we only had one twelve-inch skillet, we had to use it for everything. We could easily wipe it out with a paper towel after searing to make a quick side dish or even a sauce in the same pan.

VINNY: A lot of times, we didn't even have access to running water! We'd just wipe the skillet clean and start cooking the next dish.

Jon: One of the best things about nonstick pans is that they're totally stress-free. You don't have to worry about stuff sticking. It's a great learner's pan, too. Just remember not to get your skillet too hot before putting food in it. The skillet will start to smoke and smolder and the nonstick coating will get messed up.

VINNY: We've done that plenty of times, though! That's why we never spend big money on a nonstick. We have to replace them every couple of months anyway since we use them so often. I mean, we cook a lot of eggs, frittatas, and omelets for breakfast jobs; I've never seen anyone cook eggs in anything but a nonstick. Well, unless you're cooking them on a flat-top grill.

Jon: Do you remember when I worked at the River House in Fort Lauderdale and had to make three hundred omelets for weekend brunches?

VINNY: Yeah, and now you complain about making twenty!

Jon: Well, whether you're making one omelet or a bunch of them, what'll save you is a heat-proof silicone rubber spatula. Never, ever use anything metal on a nonstick skillet. Metal nicks up the coating, and then it becomes all gnarly and gets into the food.

VINNY: Here's a good tip: When you use heat-proof spatulas, remember that the handles aren't necessarily heat-proof. We've melted and burned the handles of so many rubber spatulas—I can't even count how many! You rest the handle on the side of the skillet, get distracted and turn around to do something else, and before you know it the handle is roached.

Jon: Nonstick isn't like a cast-iron pan that's going to gain flavor the more that it's used. The coating will eventually start to break down, so don't feel bad about replacing it. Also, if you store the skillet stacked with other pans, use paper towels as a liner so other pan bottoms don't scrape off the coating.

VINNY: Treating nonstick pans gently will definitely help you juice a few extra miles out of them.

Jon: Yeah, you definitely want to treat your nonstick well. When it comes to eggs, fish, and pan-frying, this is the skillet we go for the most.

MENU

Tortilla Española *with* MANCHEGO, Onions, *and* POTATOES

JON'S SAUSAGE, **Broccolini,** *and* **Pasta Frittata**

OUR FAVORITE **Crêpe Batter** FIVE WAYS

Basic BUTTERMILK **Pancakes**

Crunchy **Fried Feta** *and* WARM SPICED OLIVES

FRIED GOAT CHEESE, **Citrus,** *and* AVOCADO **Salad**

Spinach-Artichoke Dip *with* GRILLED BREAD

Garlicky SHRIMP CAKES *with* **Old-School** TARTAR SAUCE

SWORDFISH *with* **Fried Green Tomatoes** *and* BACON VINAIGRETTE

Crispy **Dill Snapper**

SAKE-SOY Sea Bass

Fluke *with* TARRAGON VINAIGRETTE *and* Grape Salad

Curried Chicken Nuggets *with* HONEY MUSTARD *and* Red Onion Slaw

WIENER SCHNITZEL *with* Braised RED CABBAGE

LAMB LOIN CHOPS *on* Corn Hash

BURGERS

- Jack-Bacon Burgers with Special Sauce
- Turkey-Gouda Burgers • Harissa Lamb Burgers
- Pork Burgers with Fennel-Apple Slaw and Chive Aioli

TORTILLA Española *with* Manchego, ONIONS, *and* Potatoes

3 tablespoons olive oil

2 pounds russet potatoes, peeled and sliced ⅛ inch thick

2 teaspoons kosher salt

1 yellow onion, halved and thinly sliced

1 tablespoon unsalted butter

¼ cup diced cured chorizo (not raw Mexican chorizo), optional

8 large eggs

3 tablespoons heavy cream

½ ounce grated Manchego cheese (¼ cup if using a Microplane grater)

Jon: A client of ours went crazy for tortilla Española when he was in Spain and insisted that we make it for a brunch we catered for him. We had never made one before, but since his party, we've started to make them all the time. They're so easy and delish.

VINNY: A heat-proof silicone rubber spatula is really pliant and makes getting under the eggs easy. No matter what, never use a metal spatula on a nonstick pan. It'll kill the nonstick coating.

HEAT the olive oil in a 12-inch nonstick skillet over medium-high heat. Add the potatoes and 1 teaspoon of the salt and cook until the edges of the potatoes are transparent, 5 to 7 minutes, stirring occasionally. Stir in the onions and cook for 1 minute, stirring often. Reduce the heat to medium and cook until the potatoes are tender and slightly browned, 6 to 8 minutes, stirring occasionally. Turn the potatoes and onions into a bowl and set aside. Melt the butter in the skillet, then add the chorizo and let it brown for 2 minutes. Add the potato mixture back to the skillet.

Whisk the eggs with the cream and the remaining teaspoon of salt in a medium bowl until combined. Pour over the potatoes, sprinkle with the cheese, and cook until the eggs start to set, 1 to 2 minutes. Using a heat-proof silicone rubber spatula, push the eggs to the middle of the skillet once or twice so the raw eggs on top run under the cooked eggs to the bottom of the skillet. Cook until the eggs are set on the bottom and nearly set on the top, 2 to 3 minutes.

Place a rimless plate (it should be larger in circumference than the skillet) or a large, flat pot lid on top of the skillet. Carefully flip the skillet over and lift it off; the tortilla should be on the plate. Slide the tortilla back into the skillet and cook the second side until the eggs are to your liking, 2 minutes for a soft tortilla, a minute or two longer for a hard one (we like our tortilla soft in the middle, so we cook it for less time). Slide the tortilla onto a plate and cool. Slice into wedges and serve.

SERVES 4 TO 6

JON'S SAUSAGE, BROCCOLINI, *and* Pasta Frittata

2 tablespoons unsalted butter

8 ounces raw Italian sausage, sliced ¼ inch thick

4 ounces broccolini, trimmed

1 teaspoon kosher salt

Nonstick cooking spray

8 large eggs

½ cup heavy cream

2 cups cooked tube-shaped pasta (leftover pasta works great)

¼ teaspoon red pepper flakes

2 cups Classic Marinara (see page 120), warm or at room temperature

2 ounces grated Parmigiano-Reggiano cheese (2 cups if using a Microplane grater)

Jon: I did a job in Hawaii once and the ingredients there were perversely expensive. After paying for the food, I didn't want to waste even the smallest scrap. One day, I took some pasta salad left over from the previous day and added it to the frittata that I served for lunch. The pasta was suspended in the eggs, and it looked so cool when you sliced a wedge out of the frittata. It has since become my favorite way to make frittatas.

VINNY: A cool trick is to use your convection oven option if you have one for your oven; it helps your frittata puff really high. Just turn the oven temperature down by 25°F to adjust for the circulating hot air.

PREHEAT the oven to 450°F.

Melt the butter in a large nonstick skillet over medium-high heat. Add the sausage and cook until browned, stirring often, 5 to 8 minutes. Drain the sausage on paper towels, leaving the fat in the skillet. Add the broccolini to the skillet, season with ½ teaspoon of the salt, and sauté until tender, 3 to 4 minutes. Place the broccolini on your cutting board and chop roughly. Wipe out your skillet with a paper towel.

Generously spray the skillet with nonstick cooking spray. Whisk the eggs with the cream and remaining teaspoon of salt in a medium bowl. Return the sausage and broccolini to the skillet, add an even layer of the pasta, and sprinkle with the red pepper flakes. Pour the egg mixture over evenly and place the skillet in the oven. Bake the frittata until the edges are lightly browned and puffy and the center isn't jiggly, 12 to 15 minutes.

Remove the skillet from the oven and let the frittata cool to room temperature in the skillet (it will fall as it cools). Place a plate on top of the skillet, carefully flip the skillet over, and lift it off; the frittata should be on the plate. Or you can flip the cooled frittata onto a cutting board. Slice into wedges and serve with the marinara sauce and cheese.

SERVES 4

Our FAVORITE CRÊPE BATTER FIVE WAYS

1 cup whole milk
3 large eggs
1 tablespoon vegetable oil
   plus extra as needed
½ cup all-purpose flour
Jam or Nutella spread

VINNY: You have to follow the pancake theory when making crêpes: maybe you'll mess up the first one or two, but just keep going and you'll get the hang of it.

Jon: Crêpes are so versatile. We stuff them with everything from chicken salad, to prosciutto with Fontina and arugula, to jam or Nutella, to spinach, mushrooms, and Havarti cheese. For brunches and parties, we make the crêpes ahead and rewarm them one at a time in a dry skillet.

WHISK ½ cup of the milk, the eggs, and 1 tablespoon of oil together in a large bowl. Add the flour and whisk until smooth, then whisk in the remaining ½ cup milk. Cover with plastic wrap and refrigerate for 1 hour or up to 2 days.

Brush a nonstick skillet with a little oil and set it over medium-high heat for 1 minute. Ladle about ¼ cup of batter into the skillet. Swirl the skillet to coat the pan bottom evenly and cook the batter until golden brown, 30 to 60 seconds, adjusting the heat as necessary so the crêpe doesn't get too dark.

Run a heat-proof silicone rubber spatula around the edges of the crêpe to release it from the skillet, then flip the crêpe over and brown the other side. Transfer the cooked crêpe to a plate and repeat with the remaining batter.

Spread with jam or Nutella and roll, or serve with one of the fillings opposite.

MAKES 10 CRÊPES

...VARIATIONS

FLAMING CRÊPES SUZETTE

Make one batch of crêpe batter, cook the crêpes, fold each one into quarters, and set aside.

Using the small holes of a box grater or a citrus zester, remove the zest from 2 oranges (just the zest, not the bitter white pith) and juice them to get ½ cup juice. Bring the juice and ¼ cup sugar to a simmer in a large skillet over medium-high heat. Once the sugar is dissolved, add ¼ cup Grand Marnier or Cointreau and, using a long wooden match, ignite the sauce (don't keep the open bottle of alcohol near the stove). Let the alcohol burn off, then add the zest and 2 tablespoons unsalted butter. Once the butter melts, add the folded crêpes to the skillet and turn over in the sauce to coat well. Serve topped with a scoop of vanilla ice cream.

WITH HAM AND SWISS

Make one batch of crêpe batter. While the batter rests, grate 8 ounces Gruyère cheese (about 2½ cups) and set aside.

Place 10 slices ham next to your cooktop. Cook the crêpes as described on the opposite page. After flipping each crêpe, sprinkle the cooked side with ¼ cup of the cheese and add 1 slice of the ham. Fold into thirds (like a business letter) and serve.

WITH RICOTTA AND BLUEBERRIES

Make one batch of crêpe batter, cook the crêpes, transfer to a plate, and set aside.

Stir 1½ pounds fresh ricotta together with ⅓ cup confectioners' sugar and set aside.

In a large bowl, stir together ¼ cup sugar and 1 tablespoon all-purpose flour. Add 2 pints blueberries, toss to coat, and transfer to a nonstick skillet. Add ¼ cup water, the zest and juice of 1 lemon, the seeds and pod of 1 split and scraped vanilla bean, and ¼ teaspoon vanilla extract. Simmer over low heat, stirring occasionally, until the sauce is thick, about 10 minutes. Spoon some ricotta into each crêpe, roll to enclose the filling, top with blueberry sauce, and serve.

WITH SERRANO, MAHÓN, AND MEMBRILLO (QUINCE PASTE)

Make one batch of crêpe batter. While the batter rests, grate 5 ounces of Mahón cheese (about 2 cups) and set aside.

Place 10 slices Serrano ham and 5 ounces diced quince paste (or ½ cup fig jam) next to your cooktop. Cook the crêpes as described on the opposite page. After flipping each crêpe, sprinkle the cooked side with 3 tablespoons of the cheese, some quince cubes, and 1 slice of the ham. Fold into thirds and serve.

Basic BUTTERMILK PANCAKES

3 cups buttermilk

3 large eggs, lightly beaten

3 tablespoons unsalted butter, melted

2½ cups all-purpose flour

⅓ cup sugar

1 tablespoon baking powder

1½ teaspoons baking soda

1 teaspoon kosher salt

Canola oil, as needed

fastest fruit topping
Turn 1 cup of grade-A maple syrup into a fruit topping by simmering it with 1 pint of your favorite berries. Simmer until the berries are soft, then, if they haven't broken up on their own, lightly mash them into the syrup before serving.

VINNY: Pancake parties are one of our most requested; people can choose from toppings such as old-fashioned maple syrup, fruit syrup topping (see box), crème fraîche, and even Jimmy Jon's sausage gravy (see page 214).

Jon: These pancakes are as close to perfect as a pancake can be. They're fluffy and light while still being cakey enough to earn their title. Don't get down on yourself if your first pancake or two gets screwed up. Even we mess up the first few! If you want to add fruit or chocolate chips, sprinkle them on the pancakes before you flip them; don't add extras to the batter.

WHISK together the buttermilk, eggs, and half of the melted butter in a medium bowl.

Whisk the flour, sugar, baking powder, baking soda, and salt together in a large bowl. Stir in the wet ingredients with a wooden spoon until only a few dry patches remain. Mix in the rest of the melted butter until only a few dry spots remain; the batter may be a little lumpy.

Brush a nonstick skillet with a little oil and set it over medium heat for 1 minute. Brush the skillet with a little more oil and add ¼ cup of batter for each pancake, leaving about 1½ inches between them. Cook until each pancake's surface is dotted with bubbles and the edges are dry, 2 to 3 minutes. Flip the pancakes over and cook until the other side is browned, another 2 to 3 minutes. Place the pancakes on a platter and set aside while you cook the remaining batter (brush the pan with more oil if needed), or serve the pancakes immediately with maple syrup or fruit topping.

MAKES ABOUT 1 DOZEN PANCAKES

. . . VARIATIONS

FLUFFY PANCAKES

Separate the egg yolks from the whites, and whisk the yolks with the buttermilk and all of the melted butter and set aside. Using an electric mixer or a whisk, whip the egg whites on medium-high speed until foamy, then, while beating, slowly sprinkle in 1 tablespoon of the sugar. Continue to whip the eggs until they hold medium-stiff peaks. Stir the buttermilk mixture into the dry ingredients and then whisk in one fourth of the whipped whites. Fold the remaining whipped whites into the batter with a rubber spatula (see page 212) and cook the pancakes as instructed.

JONNY 'CAKES

Substitute 1¼ cups of finely ground yellow cornmeal for 1¼ cups of the all-purpose flour. Proceed with the basic pancake recipe.

COTTAGE 'CAKES

Reduce the buttermilk from 3 cups to 2¼ cups. Along with the buttermilk mixture, stir 1½ cups of cottage cheese into the dry ingredients and proceed with the basic pancake recipe as instructed.

CRUNCHY Fried Feta and WARM SPICED OLIVES

We both have a thing for fried cheese. This crispy panko-crusted feta is amazing with the Greek salad on page 34. Or serve the fried feta solo, heaped on a plate rustic-style with lemon wedges. The olives are fantastic with a cheese tray or cocktails.

PLACE the olive oil, olives, garlic, rosemary, thyme, and red pepper flakes in a nonstick skillet over medium heat. Bring to a low simmer and cook just until the garlic is fragrant and the olives are warm, 2 to 3 minutes. Transfer to a small bowl and set aside (remove the rosemary and thyme sprigs before serving).

Place the flour in a medium bowl. Whisk the eggs with 2 tablespoons water in another bowl and place the panko in a third bowl.

Toss the feta in the flour to coat. Tap off the excess flour and then submerge all of the cubes in the egg wash. Lift the cubes out from the egg wash, letting any excess egg drip off, and place in the panko. Toss the cubes in the bread crumbs, making sure the crumbs stick to the cheese. Place the cheese cubes on a large plate and refrigerate for 30 minutes.

Heat half of the oil and half of the butter in a large nonstick skillet over medium-high heat for 2 minutes. Add about half of the breaded feta cubes and brown until golden on all sides, about 5 to 6 minutes total. Using tongs, remove the feta from the skillet and place on a paper-towel-lined plate to drain, then sprinkle with some salt. Repeat with the remaining oil, butter, and cheese. Serve hot with the warm olives.

SERVES 4

FOR THE OLIVES

2 tablespoons olive oil
1 cup mixed whole olives (we like Lucques, kalamata, and niçoise)
2 garlic cloves, roughly chopped
1 small fresh rosemary sprig
1 fresh thyme sprig
Pinch of red pepper flakes

FOR THE FETA

½ cup all-purpose flour
2 large eggs
½ cup panko bread crumbs (see Note, page 79)
10 ounces French or Greek feta, cut into 1-inch cubes
½ cup canola or grapeseed oil
2 tablespoons unsalted butter
Kosher salt

Fried GOAT CHEESE, Citrus, *and* AVOCADO SALAD

1 8-ounce goat cheese log

½ cup all-purpose flour

1 large egg

½ cup panko bread crumbs
(see Note, page 79)

½ cup canola oil

FOR THE SALAD

2 navel oranges

1 pink grapefruit

1 small shallot, finely
chopped

½ teaspoon sugar

2 tablespoons grapeseed or
canola oil

1 tablespoon extra-virgin
olive oil

Kosher salt and freshly
ground black pepper

2 cups arugula

2 Hass avocados, pitted
and thinly sliced
(see opposite)

Jon: This salad is a shout out to all of our friends and family in FLA!

VINNY: It represents the merging of our new home and our old one. From California, where we live now, we get great goat's-milk cheeses from small farms, and the country's best avocados; the best citrus comes from Florida, where we grew up.

Jon: If you can find Oro Blanco grapefruits (a hybrid between a pomelo and a grapefruit), try them. They're exceptionally sweet and not too sour.

SLICE the goat cheese into 4 rounds and shape into mini hockey pucks. Place the flour in a medium bowl. Whisk the egg with 2 tablespoons water in another bowl and place the panko in a third bowl.

Toss the goat cheese in the flour to coat. Tap off the excess flour and then submerge the cheese rounds in the egg wash. Transfer the goat cheese to the panko and press each disk in the bread crumbs, making sure the crumbs stick to the cheese. Place on a plate and refrigerate.

Following the steps in the box, opposite, remove the orange and grapefruit segments from the membrane, working over a bowl to catch the juices. Set the fruit aside. Add the shallots and sugar to 3 tablespoons of the citrus juices and whisk in the oils a little at a time. Season to taste with salt and pepper.

Divide the arugula among 4 plates. Season the avocados with some salt and pepper and add a few slices to each plate. Top with some orange and grapefruit segments.

Heat the canola oil in a large nonstick skillet over medium-high heat. Add the breaded goat cheese rounds and cook until golden brown on both sides, about 4 minutes total.

Drizzle the salads with the citrus dressing and top each with a warm goat cheese round.

SERVES 4

how to segment citrus

To segment an orange or grapefruit, slice off the top and bottom of the fruit and then, working from top to bottom, slice off the rind and bitter white pith. Separate each fruit segment from the membrane by slipping a paring knife between the fruit segment and the membrane.

how to slice an avocado

Lay an avocado on a cutting board and position your knife at the tip of the fruit. Angle the knife toward the rounded bottom of the avocado and slice down the side to the pit. Rotate the avocado, turning it against the knife, until you get to your starting point. Twist the top off from the bottom. Hit the pit with the center of your knife and then knock it off by hitting the top third of the knife against the cutting board. Peel off the skin and slice or chop as you like.

SPINACH-ARTICHOKE DIP *with* Grilled Bread

2 tablespoons unsalted butter

6 garlic cloves, finely chopped

1 15-ounce can water-packed artichoke hearts, drained and quartered

6 ounces chopped fresh spinach (about 4 cups)

8 ounces cream cheese

½ to ¾ cup grated Parmigiano-Reggiano cheese

1 teaspoon kosher salt

1 baguette, sliced ⅓ inch thick on a diagonal

6 tablespoons olive oil

This dip is so easy to make. Room-temperature cream cheese is a little easier to work into the artichokes and spinach, but it works fine with cream cheese straight from the fridge, too.

MELT the butter in a large nonstick skillet over medium-high heat. Add the garlic and cook until it becomes fragrant, 30 seconds to 1 minute. Add the artichokes and the spinach and cook, stirring often, until the spinach wilts, 3 minutes.

Stir in the cream cheese and mix until it is thoroughly combined with the spinach and artichokes (if the mixture seems tight, add a tablespoon or two of water). Mix in the Parmigiano-Reggiano and salt, and scrape the dip into a serving bowl.

Wipe the skillet clean and place over medium-high heat. Drizzle or brush both sides of the bread with the olive oil. Toast the bread in the skillet in batches until both sides are golden, 3 to 4 minutes total (or toast the bread in a 400°F oven). Serve the toasted bread with the dip.

SERVES 8

---

grating cheese

There are lots of kitchen tools you can use to grate cheese: the small holes of a box grater, a fine Microplane grater (this tends to make fluffy ribbons of cheese), or even a food processor fitted with the grater attachment or not (sometimes we just toss a chunk of Parm into the food processor and let 'er rip until it's finely ground). Different ways of grating will give you a different yield, but don't worry about it too much; we've never heard anyone complaining of too much cheese!

GARLICKY Shrimp Cakes *with* Old-School TARTAR SAUCE

FOR THE TARTAR SAUCE

1 cup mayonnaise

1 hard-boiled egg, peeled and finely chopped

2 tablespoons drained capers (rinsed if salt-packed)

2 tablespoons sweet pickle relish

1 teaspoon Tabasco sauce

1 teaspoon Worcestershire sauce

FOR THE SHRIMP CAKES

½ cup heavy cream

1 shallot, halved and thinly sliced

3 garlic cloves, smashed

½ pound raw shrimp (any size), shelled, deveined, and finely chopped

½ red onion, finely diced

1 small celery stalk, very finely diced

¼ cup finely chopped fresh flat-leaf parsley

1 teaspoon finely chopped fresh thyme

1 teaspoon kosher salt

1 large egg

2 cups panko bread crumbs (see Note, page 79)

½ to ¾ cup canola oil

Jon: Most of the raw shrimp you get today at the grocery store is flash-frozen, and you never know for sure how many hours the shrimp has been sitting out. To be sure the shrimp is still good, smell it before you use it. If it doesn't smell right, toss it. Or, avoid this scenario and buy frozen shrimp and defrost them on your own schedule.

VINNY: Get your oil super hot, otherwise your shrimp cakes turn into a sponge and instead of frying, they will just soak up a lot of oil and be really greasy.

TO make the tartar sauce, stir together all of the ingredients in a small bowl. Cover with plastic wrap and refrigerate until ready to serve (the sauce can be made a few days in advance).

Bring the cream, shallots, and garlic to a gentle simmer in a nonstick skillet over medium heat. Reduce the heat to a bare simmer and cook, stirring occasionally, until the cream is reduced to ¼ cup, 6 to 8 minutes. Pour the cream through a fine-mesh sieve and into a small bowl and set aside to cool.

Mix the shrimp, onions, celery, all but 1 tablespoon of the parsley, thyme, and salt in a large bowl. Whisk the egg into the cooled cream and stir it into the shrimp, then mix in ¾ cup of the panko. Use 2 tablespoons of the shrimp mixture (more for a larger cake) to form each shrimp patty. Place the remaining 1¼ cups of panko in a shallow dish and dip each shrimp cake in the panko, pressing the bread crumbs on to make sure they stick. Place the cakes on a baking sheet and refrigerate for at least 30 minutes or up to 4 hours.

Heat the canola oil in a large nonstick skillet over medium-high heat until it's really hot (about 350°F). Add a few cakes (don't overcrowd the pan) and fry until golden brown on both sides, about 8 minutes, adjusting the heat as necessary so the cakes don't get too dark too quickly. Serve hot, with some tartar sauce on the side. Garnish with the reserved chopped parsley.

MAKES 9 TO 10 CAKES

tip

How do you know when your oil is hot? Make a sacrifice to the skillet! Add a bread cube; the oil surrounding it should immediately sizzle and bubble around it. If it doesn't, carefully remove the cube of bread and let the oil get hotter. If the oil vigorously bubbles and spurts when you add the cube, then your oil is too hot; again, carefully remove the bread and lower the heat. Or, invest in an inexpensive digital thermometer that will tell you when the oil is at 350°F.

SWORDFISH *with* Fried Green Tomatoes *and* BACON VINAIGRETTE

1 large egg

2 firm green tomatoes, sliced ½ inch thick

½ cup all-purpose flour

½ cup cornmeal

5 tablespoons canola or grapeseed oil

5 tablespoons unsalted butter

1½ teaspoons kosher salt

4 6- to 8-ounce swordfish steaks

Warm Bacon Vinaigrette (page 42)

Jon: We both grew up in Florida, where food is heavily influenced by neighboring states. If you leave out the swordfish here, you have a real classic Southern side dish that would kill with pork chops or fried chicken.

VINNY: Swordfish has an amazing steaky quality that works nicely with the tenderness of fried tomatoes. If your market doesn't sell sustainably caught wild swordfish, use catfish or tilapia in its place.

WHISK the egg with 2 tablespoons water in a small dish. Dredge each tomato slice in the flour, tapping off any excess, and then dip it into the egg wash, letting the excess egg drip off before dredging it through the cornmeal. Repeat with the remaining slices.

Heat 2 tablespoons of the oil with 2 tablespoons of the butter in a nonstick skillet over medium-high heat until the butter is melted. Once melted, continue to heat for another 30 seconds and then add half of the tomato slices and fry on both sides until golden brown and crispy, 2 to 4 minutes. Transfer to a paper-towel-lined plate and sprinkle with ¼ teaspoon of the salt. Repeat with the remaining tomatoes.

Sprinkle both sides of the swordfish with the remaining 1 teaspoon of salt. Wipe out the skillet with paper towels. Add the remaining 3 tablespoons of oil and 3 tablespoons of butter to the pan. Once the butter is melted, add the fish. Sear both sides until browned and cooked through, 10 to 12 minutes total. Serve with the fried green tomatoes and drizzle with the bacon vinaigrette.

SERVES 4

CRISPY Dill SNAPPER

VINNY: Using another pan to weight down fish so it cooks flat and doesn't curl is a great restaurant trick that transfers to home kitchens. Make sure that the pan you use to weight down the fish is completely cool; a hot pan (such as one that was sitting on the cooktop of your stove) will stick to the flesh of the fish.

Jon: Take a sip of the wine you're going to cook with, get loose, and envision the dish. You want a nice crisp and dry white wine to play off of the dill. Always cook with wine that is good enough to drink solo.

4 6- to 8-ounce red snapper fillets (sea bass is great, too)

1½ teaspoons kosher salt

2 tablespoons canola or grapeseed oil

⅔ cup dry white wine (such as pinot grigio or sauvignon blanc)

1 tablespoon white wine vinegar

1 large shallot, halved and thinly sliced

1 tablespoon grainy mustard

4 whole black peppercorns

⅓ cup heavy cream

4 tablespoons (½ stick) unsalted butter, quartered

1 tablespoon finely chopped fresh dill

USING a paring knife, make 3 diagonal slashes in the skin of each fish fillet, being careful not to cut into the fish. Use 1 teaspoon of the salt to season the fish on both sides and set aside.

Heat a nonstick skillet with the 2 tablespoons of oil over medium-high heat for 2 minutes (if your skillet isn't big enough to comfortably hold all 4 fillets at once, then fry the fish in batches and heat only 1 tablespoon of oil before adding the fillets). Place the fish in the skillet, skin side down, and place a smaller heavy skillet or pot on top to weight it down. Sear the fish until the edges are golden brown and crisp, 3 to 4 minutes. Turn the fish over, weight it down again, and cook the other side until it is browned and the fish is cooked through, another 2 to 3 minutes. Transfer the fish to a platter. (If frying in batches, keep the first 2 fillets warm on a rimmed sheet pan in a 250°F oven while you fry the remainder.)

Add the white wine, vinegar, shallots, mustard, and peppercorns to the skillet and cook until the liquid is reduced to ¼ cup, 2 to 3 minutes. Stir in the cream and continue to simmer, stirring often, until the cream is thick, another 2 to 3 minutes. Stir in the butter, dill, and remaining ½ teaspoon salt. Once the butter is melted, pour the sauce over the fish and serve.

SERVES 4

SAKE-SOY Sea Bass

1 2-inch piece of fresh ginger,
peeled and sliced into
¼-inch-thick rounds

1 cup mirin (sweetened rice
wine)

1 cup sake

½ cup soy sauce

2 stalks lemongrass, trimmed,
tough outer layer
removed, sliced ¼ inch
thick and smashed

2 shallots, halved and thinly
sliced

4 garlic cloves, smashed

4 6-ounce sea bass fillets

2 tablespoons grapeseed oil

Pinch of kosher salt

tip
Ginger is the most tender right beneath its skin. Peel your ginger with a metal spoon to scrape away just the papery peel and nothing else.

Smashing the individual pieces of ginger and lemongrass may seem like a waste of time, but it's not: by smashing them (like garlic) you release their intensely fragrant essential oils. This fish tastes best if you can marinate it for at least four hours or overnight before cooking.

PLACE the ginger rounds on a cutting board and with the flat side of a chef's knife, smash them to release their essential oils. Transfer them to a small bowl and stir in the mirin, sake, soy sauce, lemongrass, shallots, and garlic. Set aside ¼ cup for the sauce and transfer the rest to a resealable plastic bag. Add the fish to the bag and refrigerate for at least 4 hours or overnight.

Heat the oil in a nonstick skillet over medium-high heat. Lightly season the fish with salt and sear until golden brown, about 4 minutes (if using a smaller skillet, cook the fish in two batches). Flip and cook until the other side has color and the fish is cooked to your preference. We like to cook it another 3 to 4 minutes so it stays medium-rare (if cooked until well done, it could be difficult to transfer in one piece to a plate). Transfer the fish to a plate and set aside.

Wipe the skillet with a paper towel and add the ¼ cup of reserved marinade. Simmer over high heat until it thickens, 1 to 2 minutes. Spoon the sauce over the fish and serve.

SERVES 4

+ 1 pan:
baby bok choy
Baby bok choy makes a good side dish for fish. Just blanch 8 halved heads (slice the whole head in half, lengthwise) in boiling, salted water for 2 to 3 minutes until tender, drain, and serve.

FLUKE *with* Tarragon Vinaigrette *and* GRAPE SALAD

VINNY: Any flaky fish works well here. We like fluke because it's usually a little less pricey than its cousin, flounder. If fluke isn't available at your market, feel free to sub in flounder, tilapia, or sole.

Jon: I love pepper in ranch dressing (see page 44) and pasta carbonara (see page 154), but not over a beautiful, pristine, fresh-caught fish fillet! If you sprinkle fish with pepper, it will taste like pepper, and this is such a delicate fish dish that pepper just gets in the way.

WHISK all of the vinaigrette ingredients in a small bowl and set aside.

To make the salad, whisk the chervil, chives, lemon juice, and olive oil together in a medium bowl. Add the grapes and gently toss to coat. Divide among four plates and set aside.

Heat 2 tablespoons of the oil in a large nonstick skillet over medium-high heat. Sprinkle the fluke fillets with the salt. Add 2 fluke fillets and sear until golden brown, 3 to 5 minutes (less for thinner fillets, longer for thicker ones). Use a fish spatula to turn over and sear the other side until browned, another 2 to 4 minutes. Transfer the fish to a plate and repeat with the remaining fillets, adding more oil as needed. Drizzle each fillet with some vinaigrette and serve.

SERVES 4

FOR THE VINAIGRETTE

2 tablespoons white wine vinegar

2 tablespoons grapeseed or canola oil

1½ tablespoons extra-virgin olive oil

½ small shallot, minced

1 tablespoon finely chopped fresh tarragon

1½ teaspoons finely chopped fresh thyme

1½ teaspoons grainy mustard

Juice of ½ lemon

1½ teaspoons sugar

¼ teaspoon kosher salt

FOR THE SALAD

1 teaspoon finely chopped fresh chervil

¼ teaspoon finely chopped fresh chives, plus a few sprigs for garnish

½ teaspoon fresh lemon juice

¼ teaspoon olive oil

1 cup halved black or red seedless grapes

¼ cup grapeseed or canola oil

4 6-ounce fluke fillets

1½ teaspoons kosher salt

Curried **Chicken Nuggets** *with* HONEY MUSTARD *and* Red Onion SLAW

FOR THE HONEY MUSTARD

¼ cup Gulden's mustard

½ cup mayonnaise

3 tablespoons honey

FOR THE RED ONION SLAW

½ red onion, thinly sliced

1 pint cherry or grape
tomatoes, halved

1 cup watercress, tough stems
removed

½ cup finely chopped fresh
cilantro

Juice of 2 to 3 limes

2 tablespoons olive oil

½ teaspoon kosher salt

FOR THE NUGGETS

1 cup panko bread crumbs
(see Note, opposite)

¾ cup all-purpose flour

1½ tablespoons curry powder

1 tablespoon turmeric

1½ teaspoons cayenne pepper

1½ teaspoons ground cumin

1 teaspoon ground coriander

4 boneless, skinless chicken
breasts

1 cup canola oil

Kosher salt

Every kid we know (and a lot of adults, too) loves chicken nuggets. This is our homemade version. Panko bread crumbs are a find; they don't absorb as much grease as regular bread crumbs do, and they stay crispy for a while after the food is fried.

TO make the honey mustard, mix the mustard, mayonnaise, and honey together in a small bowl and set aside (this can be made up to 2 or 3 days in advance).

To make the red onion slaw, combine the onions, tomatoes, watercress, and cilantro in a medium bowl. Sprinkle with lime juice, olive oil, and salt, toss together, and set aside.

To make the nuggets, whisk the panko, flour, and spices together in a large bowl. Cut the chicken into 1-inch chunks, and toss in the mixture to coat.

Heat the canola oil in a large nonstick skillet until hot (350°F). Fry half of the nuggets until golden brown on all sides, 5 to 6 minutes total. Transfer to a paper-towel-lined plate, season with salt, and repeat with the remaining chicken. (If you like you can place the cooked nuggets on a rimmed sheet pan and keep them warm in a 250°F oven.) Serve with the honey mustard and the slaw.

SERVES 4

...VARIATION

CURRIED TOFU NUGGETS

Substitute 1 pound of drained firm tofu for the chicken. Slice into 1½-inch cubes and place them on a paper-towel-lined plate to absorb excess moisture. Follow the breading and frying instructions as described.

note

We use Japanese panko bread crumbs all the time because we like their neutral flavor and lightness. However, panko bread crumbs come in fairly rough flakes, whereas we prefer a finer crumb, so we give them a whirl in the food processor. We'll do this in big batches, and then store the finely ground panko in a resealable bag or airtight container so we're always stocked and ready to go, whether we're making meatloaf or breading fillets.

WIENER SCHNITZEL *with* BRAISED Red Cabbage

FOR THE RED CABBAGE

2 dried juniper berries (optional)

2 whole cloves

1 bay leaf

1 cinnamon stick

6 bacon strips, halved lengthwise and sliced crosswise into ¼-inch-thick strips

1 onion, finely chopped

1 Granny Smith apple, peeled, cored, and diced

¼ cup dry red wine

3 tablespoons red wine vinegar

¼ cup red currant jelly

1 bunch curly parsley, chopped, plus a few sprigs for garnish

1 tablespoon sugar

1 small head of red cabbage, quartered, cored, and very thinly sliced crosswise

½ teaspoon arrowroot or cornstarch, dissolved in 1 tablespoon water

½ teaspoon kosher salt

1 cup all-purpose flour

1 cup panko bread crumbs

2 large eggs

1 pound ¼-inch-thick veal cutlets

½ cup canola oil

2 teaspoons kosher salt

Jon: Veal tenderloin makes tender schnitzel, but if you don't want to swallow the cost of it, use a cheaper cut, such as veal loin. If veal isn't your thing, go for chicken or pork cutlets.

VINNY: The addition of curly parsley gives this recipe a cool old-school effect.

TO make the cabbage, place the juniper berries (if using), cloves, bay leaf, and cinnamon stick in a tea ball and set aside. (If you don't have a tea ball, you can add the spices directly to the cabbage; just fish them out before serving.)

Place the bacon in a nonstick skillet and cook over medium-high heat until browned and crispy, stirring occasionally, about 7 minutes. Add the onions and cook until they are limp and transparent, about 3 minutes. Stir in the apples, ½ cup water, the wine, vinegar, jelly, chopped parsley, and sugar and cook, stirring, for 1 minute. Add the tea ball (or loose spices) and cook for another 2 minutes. Stir in the cabbage, reduce the heat to medium, cover the skillet, and cook until the cabbage is tender and there is about ¼ inch of liquid left in the pan, another 30 minutes (check the cabbage a few times throughout to make sure the liquid hasn't evaporated; if the liquid level gets low, add ¼ cup water to the skillet). Remove the tea ball and stir in the arrowroot or cornstarch paste. Cook until the cabbage gets a glazed look, about 2 minutes longer. Season with the salt and transfer to a covered serving dish to stay warm. Wipe out the skillet and set aside.

Place the flour and panko on 2 separate plates. Whisk the eggs with 3 tablespoons water in a medium bowl. Dredge each cutlet through the flour to coat, tapping off the excess. Submerge in the egg wash, then transfer to the panko and press the bread crumbs into the cutlet, making sure they stick to the meat.

Heat the oil in a nonstick skillet over medium-high heat. Place 2 cutlets in the pan, reduce the heat to medium, and gently brown on both sides, 5 to 6 minutes total. Transfer to a paper-towel-lined plate to drain and immediately sprinkle with some of the salt. Repeat with the remaining cutlets. Garnish with sprigs of parsley and serve with the braised red cabbage on the side.

SERVES 4

thick, not pasty

Arrowroot is a white powder used to thicken sauces. Unlike cornstarch, it leaves sauces perfectly clear and without a hint of pastiness. We think it offers a much cleaner flavor and appearance than cornstarch can, but if you can't find it, cornstarch will work out fine.

LAMB LOIN CHOPS
on *CORN* Hash

5 tablespoons canola or
   grapeseed oil

1 large Yukon Gold or russet
   potato, peeled and diced
   into ½-inch cubes

1½ teaspoons kosher salt

1 fennel bulb, fronds and
   stalks removed, cored and
   finely chopped

1 large yellow onion, finely
   chopped

3 ears of corn, kernels sliced
   off the cob

3 tablespoons finely chopped
   roasted red peppers (from
   a jar is fine)

2 teaspoons finely chopped
   fresh chives

1½ teaspoons finely chopped
   fresh flat-leaf parsley

4 1½- to 2-inch-thick lamb
   loin chops

FOR THE SAUCE

½ small shallot, finely
   chopped

1½ teaspoons sugar

¼ teaspoon salt

½ cup dry sherry

4 tablespoons (½ stick)
   unsalted butter

Jon: Lamb loin chops are the most tender and leanest type of lamb chop. They're best kept medium-rare, otherwise they can take on a strong gamy flavor.

VINNY: For the sweetest result, it's important to cook corn the same day you buy it. Wipe out the corn's residue from the skillet before adding the chops, because the sugars can burn.

HEAT 2 tablespoons of the oil in a nonstick skillet over medium-high heat for 2 minutes. Add the potatoes and cook, stirring occasionally, until golden brown and cooked through, about 5 minutes. Transfer to a large bowl, season with ½ teaspoon of the salt, and set aside.

Reduce the heat to medium and add 2 more tablespoons of the oil, the fennel, and the onions. Cook until caramelized, soft, and brown, 10 to 12 minutes, and then season with ½ teaspoon of salt. Transfer to the bowl with the potatoes and add the corn to the skillet. Cook the corn until tender, about 3 minutes, and add to the bowl with the vegetables along with the peppers, chives, and parsley. Turn the heat to low and use paper towels to quickly wipe out the skillet.

Sprinkle the lamb chops with the remaining ½ teaspoon of salt. Add the remaining 1 tablespoon of oil to the skillet, increase the heat to medium-high, and sear the lamb until browned on each side, 6 to 8 minutes total. Transfer to a plate and set aside while you make the sauce.

Drain off any fat in the pan and reduce the heat to medium. Add the shallots, sugar, salt, and sherry. Cook for 2 to 3 minutes or until the liquid is reduced by half. Swirl in the butter. Taste for seasoning, pour over the lamb chops, and serve.

SERVES 4

CAST IRON

Jon: This is probably my favorite pan of all. It conducts heat evenly and it's easy to clean. You can get a solid sear off of it and pick up the most amazing colors and deep chars. It's just awesome. If you don't have one, go buy one now—and make our buttermilk-brined fried chicken the first recipe you try. It will blow you away.

VINNY: Take it from me, you don't want to get between Jonny and his fried chicken!

Jon: I have good reason: a cast-iron pan is the best for frying. It conducts such even heat, and retains heat, too. Plus, there's something really cool about cooking fried chicken in cast iron. It's so down-home, you know?

VINNY: Totally agree, plus you can do so many other things in it, too, like searing chops, or caramelizing onions . . . you can even make eggs in it! Also, they transfer from stovetop to oven with no plastic handles to worry about. If treated well, a cast-iron skillet takes on a coating similar to that of a non-stick pan. Plus you get an added benefit of a little extra iron cooked into your food. A twelve-inch skillet is your best all-around all-purpose size, so start with that.

Jon: Traditionally, cast iron is cleaned with just really hot water and a scrub pad. We use ours so often, though, that we clean them out with soap, too. If you decide to clean yours with soap (preferably diluted dish soap) you really should reseason it before using it again: heat the skillet over high heat for a couple of minutes, add a tablespoon or two of oil, let it warm for a minute or two, then turn off the heat, let the pan cool, and wipe out the excess. Or put it upside down on the rack of a warm oven for 30 minutes or so, then set upright to cool.

VINNY: If you just use hot water to clean out your cast iron, be sure to dry it thoroughly before putting it away. Cast iron is porous, and water can seep into it and rust. Then your cast-iron pan is done.

Jon: To get off any burnt-on bits without scouring or using soap, clean your cast iron with kosher salt. When the pan is cold, fill it with about $\frac{1}{2}$ inch of salt and set it over high heat. Once the salt starts to smoke, use a wooden spoon to push it around the skillet, scraping it against the bottom of the pan. Let it go for a minute or two, then turn off the heat and let the pan (and the salt) cool down. That salt is screaming hot—whatever you do, don't touch it until it has cooled down!

VINNY: A cast-iron pan can last you a lifetime. If you see one at a flea market or yard sale, grab it. Chances are that it has been put through its paces by someone's grandma and it's all primed and ready to go.

Jon: Yeah, cast iron is like a fine bottle of wine. The older it is, the better it gets.

some recipes that work great in a cast-iron skillet are:

- Swordfish with Fried Green Tomatoes and Bacon Vinaigrette, page 72
- Crispy Dill Snapper, page 73
- Lamb Loin Chops on Corn Hash, opposite
- Grouper with Lemon-Caper Butter, page 104
- Chicken Provençal, page 113
- Spicy Citrus-Glazed Duck Breasts, page 116
- Ricotta- and Pancetta-Stuffed Pork Chops, page 118
- Tri-Tips with Salsa Verde, page 122
- Buttermilk-Sage Fried Chicken, page 152

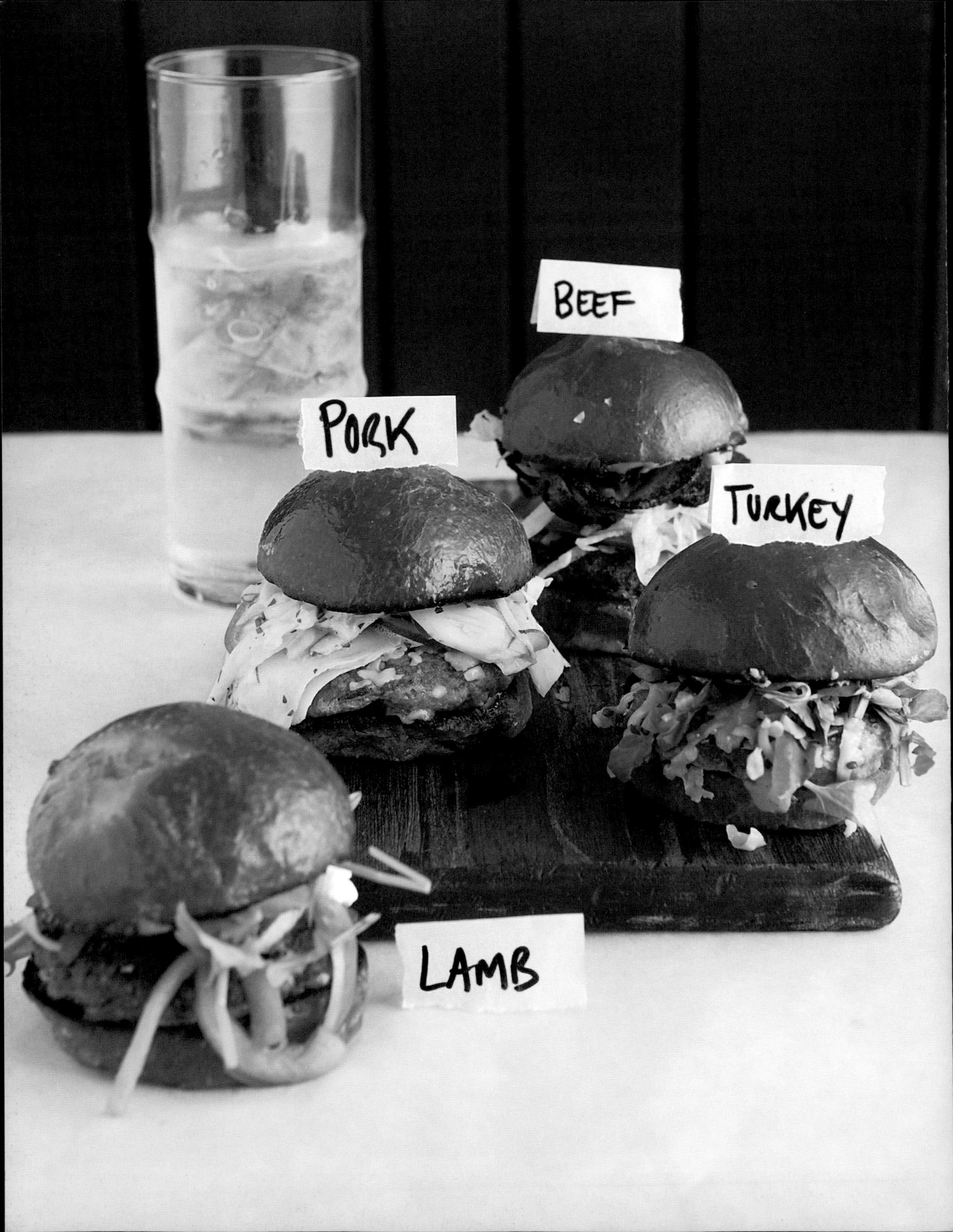
BEEF
PORK
TURKEY
LAMB

BURGERS

Jon: Everyone loves a good burger, whether they eat beef or not. Even here in health-conscious Los Angeles there's intense burger competition at all levels, from fast-food joints to high-end restaurants. I think it's because a good burger is so pleasing no matter how much you paid for it.

VINNY: That said, the best burger is probably one that you make yourself because you can control the quality of the meat, how it's shaped, how it's cooked, the condiments, and the bun.

Jon: Flimsy burger buns are fine for back-yard barbecues, but we prefer sturdy rolls—especially brioche rolls—to traditional buns ninety-nine percent of the time. They're tender and light, and they don't fall apart.

VINNY: When it comes to the meat itself, it's important not to pack it too much, not to overhandle it. Just gently shape it into a patty (see below for shaping tips).

Jon: We've never been fans of seasoning the meat; we prefer to use great-quality meat, and top it with interesting condiments.

VINNY: Otherwise, your burger ends up tasting like a sausage!

shaping burgers

Free-form patties are homey, but they don't cook evenly and usually puff up a lot in the middle. That's why we like to use a mold to shape our burgers.

One way to do it is to use the lid of a plastic container, such as a peanut butter jar or mayonnaise jar. Line the inside with plastic wrap, lightly press in the meat, and then turn it out.

For a thicker burger, try using a block of Styrofoam. Cut a circle (or square) out of the Styrofoam. Line it with a long sheet of plastic wrap, lightly pack in the meat, and then use the overhang to lift the burger out of the mold.

No matter what you do, don't overpack your burgers. A loosely packed burger tends to be more tender and juicy.

Jack-Bacon BURGERS *with* SPECIAL Sauce

FOR THE SPECIAL SAUCE

½ cup ketchup

½ cup mayonnaise

1½ tablespoons sweet pickle relish

1½ tablespoons Worcestershire sauce

1½ teaspoons finely ground black pepper

FOR THE BURGERS

12 slices bacon (preferably applewood smoked)

2 white or yellow onions, finely diced

2 pounds ground chuck or sirloin

2 teaspoons kosher salt

2 tablespoons canola or grapeseed oil

1 cup grated Monterey Jack cheese

4 burger buns (preferably brioche)

2 tablespoons unsalted butter, at room temperature

1 large tomato, sliced

1 head of butter lettuce (such as Bibb or Boston), thinly sliced crosswise into ribbons

Jon: I can occasionally get into a lamb burger or a pork one, but to me, there's no burger better than your traditional hamburger.

VINNY: Grated cheese is excellent on burgers. The part of the cheese that touches the hot burger and bun gets nice and soft, while the inner cheese core retains a colder temp and its shredded texture. Piling on a grated mound rather than using a slice also really allows the flavor and texture of the cheese to come through.

STIR the ingredients for the sauce in a small bowl and refrigerate until serving (or up to 1 week).

Heat a large nonstick skillet over medium-high heat for 1 minute. Add the bacon (cook the bacon in two batches if your pan isn't big enough) and cook until both sides are browned and crispy, about 10 minutes total. Set aside on a paper-towel-lined plate.

Add the onions to the skillet, reduce the heat to medium, and cook, stirring occasionally, until they are caramelized, 10 to 12 minutes. Transfer the onions to a small bowl and set aside. Wipe out the skillet with a paper towel and set aside.

Place the meat in a large bowl and, using your hands, work in the salt. Form the meat into 4 patties (see page 85 for shaping tips). Add the oil to the skillet and place over medium-high heat. When hot, add the burgers and cook until browned on one side, 3 to 4 minutes.

Flip the burgers and pile a small mound of cheese on top of each, cooking until the second side is browned, another 2 to 3 minutes. Cut a small slit into the center of one of the burgers to check the color for doneness. Place the burgers on a platter and set aside.

Wipe out your skillet with a paper towel. Spread the cut side of each bun with some softened butter and place them cut side down in the pan. Cook until lightly toasted.

Spread some Special Sauce on the top half of each bun and place a burger on the bottom half. Top the burger with some onions, a tomato slice, and some bacon and lettuce, and serve immediately.

MAKES 4 BURGERS

tip

Special Sauce is always in our fridge. It's killer on a BLT sandwich, the Carmelized Productions house favorite, and is also great instead of ketchup with fries or chicken fingers.

TURKEY-GOUDA Burgers

1¾ pounds ground turkey

2 teaspoons kosher salt

2 tablespoons canola or
grapeseed oil

1 cup grated Gouda cheese

4 burger buns (preferably
brioche)

2 tablespoons unsalted butter,
at room temperature

2 tablespoons grainy mustard

½ medium red onion, thinly
sliced

1 cup watercress, thick stems
removed

freezing buns

Here's a cool trick of the trade: buy brioche buns in bulk, and wrap each one individually in plastic wrap before freezing and transferring to a larger bag. The buns stay nice and fresh and you're always ready for burger action. Keep in mind that when freezing buns, it's nice to warm them up before serving. A little soft butter and a hot skillet or grill really brings them back to life.

Jon: Roasted turkey is typically so dry, which is why good gravy is key on Thanksgiving. Ground turkey meat tends to retain more moisture, making for a juicier end product (no gravy necessary).

VINNY: For an extra-juicy burger, I like to blend some ground dark turkey meat into the white ground turkey meat. This burger is also tasty with the chive aioli on page 90.

PLACE the meat in a large bowl and use your hands to work in the salt. Form the meat into 4 patties (see page 85 for shaping tips).

Add the oil to a large nonstick skillet and place over medium-high heat. When hot, add the burgers, cover, and cook until browned, 6 to 8 minutes. Flip the burgers and cook, covered, for 4 minutes longer. Pile a small mound of cheese on top of each burger and continue to fry, covered, until the burger is cooked through and the bottom is browned, another 2 to 4 minutes. Place the burgers on a platter and set aside.

Wipe out your skillet with a paper towel. Spread the cut side of each bun with some softened butter, then place them cut side down in the pan and cook until lightly toasted.

Spread some mustard on the top half of each bun and place a burger on the bottom half. Top the burger with red onions, watercress, and the top bun and serve.

MAKES 4 BURGERS

HARISSA Lamb Burgers

Jon: We're constantly scouring supermarkets and specialty stores for cool new ingredients, and harissa—a hot and spicy chile-garlic sauce from North Africa—is one we stumbled upon years ago. Since then, the response for anything we make with harissa has been through the roof. People love it—especially with lamb.

VINNY: Lamb burgers are rich and bold, like beef, but more exotic. Try substituting ground buffalo meat for the lamb for something a little different.

STIR the aioli ingredients together in a small bowl and refrigerate until serving (or up to 2 days).

Place the meat in a large bowl and use your hands to work in the salt. Form the meat into 4 patties (see shaping tips on page 85). Add the oil to a large nonstick skillet over medium-high heat and cook the burgers, covered, until browned, 3 to 4 minutes. Flip the burgers and cook, covered, until your desired degree of doneness, another 2 to 3 minutes. Place the burgers on a platter and set aside.

Wipe out your skillet with a paper towel. Spread the cut side of each bun with some softened butter, then place them cut side down in the pan and cook until lightly toasted.

Spread some aioli on the top half of each bun and place a burger on the bottom half. Top the burger with some pickled onions, feta, and arugula, add the top bun, and serve.

MAKES 4 BURGERS

FOR THE HARISSA AIOLI

1 cup mayonnaise
½ cup prepared harissa
3 tablespoons ketchup

FOR THE BURGERS

1¾ pounds ground lamb
2 teaspoons kosher salt
2 tablespoons canola or grapeseed oil
6 burger buns (preferably brioche)
2 tablespoons unsalted butter, at room temperature
1 recipe Pickled Red Onions (page 34)
½ cup crumbled feta cheese
2 cups arugula

Pork Burgers *with* FENNEL-APPLE **Slaw** *and* CHIVE AIOLI

FOR THE CHIVE AIOLI

½ cup mayonnaise

1 tablespoon cider vinegar

1 tablespoon finely chopped
fresh chives

1½ teaspoons Dijon mustard

1½ teaspoons honey

¼ teaspoon kosher salt

FOR THE SLAW

2 apples (preferably
Braeburn, Gala, or Pink
Lady), peeled, cored,
quartered, and very thinly
sliced

1 fennel bulb, fronds and
stalks removed, cored and
thinly sliced

½ small red onion, very
thinly sliced

¼ head of green cabbage,
thinly sliced crosswise

2 jalapeños, seeded,
deveined, and thinly
sliced

¼ cup finely chopped fresh
flat-leaf parsley

1 teaspoon kosher salt

Jon: Our pork burgers are definitely a little more adventurous than a burger with cheese and sauce. The sweetness of the fennel and apples plays off of the richness of the pork and the tangy aioli. We love them, especially when kept slightly pink in the middle so they're still juicy.

VINNY: For super-thin slices of fennel and red onions, we use a mandoline. It's an extra piece of equipment, but if you really get down on this slaw, then it's worth the investment.

STIR the aioli ingredients together in a small bowl and refrigerate until serving (or up to 2 days).

Mix the slaw ingredients together in a large bowl. Stir in 2 tablespoons of the aioli (refrigerate the rest for later), cover the slaw with plastic wrap, and refrigerate until you're ready to serve the burgers.

Place the meat in a large bowl and use your hands to work in the salt. Form the meat into 4 patties (see page 85 for shaping tips). Add the oil to a large nonstick skillet and place over medium-high heat. When hot, add the burgers and cook, covered, until browned, 3 to 4 minutes. Flip the burgers and place a small mound of cheese on top of each. Cook, covered, until the underside is browned, another 2 to 3 minutes longer. Cut a small slit into one of the burgers; the juices should run light pink. If necessary cook the burgers for another few minutes to reach the desired doneness. Place the burgers on a platter and set aside.

FOR THE BURGERS

1¾ pounds ground pork

2 teaspoons kosher salt

2 tablespoons canola or grapeseed oil

1 cup shredded sharp white Cheddar cheese

4 burger buns (preferably brioche)

2 tablespoons unsalted butter, at room temperature

Wipe out your skillet with a paper towel. Spread the cut side of each bun with some softened butter, then place them cut side down in the pan and cook until lightly toasted.

Spread some aioli on the top half of each bun and place a burger on the bottom half. Top the burger with some slaw and serve.

MAKES 4 BURGERS

mini burgers

We're known for our mini burgers. They're great for parties because they're easy to eat, and people can dig into a three-bite burger and still have an appetite for the rest of the meal to come. Minis are also cool to serve as sets, for example, one mini beef, one mini turkey, and one mini lamb. If you can't find mini brioche buns, substitute a dinner roll. You can even use a biscuit cutter to trim the roll down to size. There's nothing worse than when your mini gets lost in the bun!

CLASSIC SKILLET/ FRYING PAN

Jon: A traditional stainless skillet (including clad metal pans made from aluminum and stainless steel) is one of the most commonly used pans in restaurant and home kitchens.

VINNY: It's without a doubt the pan that I most often grab when I need to cook something on the stovetop.

Jon: Unlike cast-irons and nonsticks, you can build really flavorful sauces in a traditional skillet. The brown stuff at the bottom of the pan that's left after the meat is seared is called the *fond*; it's where all the flavor is. When you go to scrape the bottom of the pan after adding wine or tomatoes, the *fond* mingles in with the liquid, giving it a deep and rich taste.

VINNY: This is definitely your go-to pan if you're making a pan sauce. Because nothing sticks to a nonstick, you don't get that *fond* on the bottom of the skillet and you can't build a pan sauce with nice depth of flavor. And cream-based sauces don't work so well in a cast-iron pan. We find the flavor coming from a stainless skillet is much cleaner.

Jon: When cooking with a stainless skillet, be sure to scrub off any browned-on bits thoroughly when you're cleaning the pan. Any black stuff left in the pan can mess up the flavor of whatever you're cooking next, make ingredients you're cooking stick and burn, or contribute a bitter taste to the food and make your kitchen really smoky—or all of the above.

VINNY: If you burn stuff onto the pan, soak it in soapy water and scrub it out. If that doesn't work, then fill the pan with a little water, bring the water to a boil, then let the pan sit on the stovetop until the water is lukewarm. You'll be able to scrape off that scuzz with a steel-wool pad. Bon Ami and Bar Keeper's Friend, both powder cleansers, also work well.

Jon: When you're buying a stainless skillet, be sure to choose one that transfers from the stovetop to the oven.

VINNY: You want the flexibility of being able to finish a dish off in the oven (such as our stuffed pork chops on page 118). If your skillet has a plastic handle that can melt, you won't be able to do that.

Jon: For even browning and heat distribution, buy a pan with a thick bottom; thin sides are okay, but you want the base of the pan to be solid so whatever you're searing in the pan doesn't get scorched.

MENU

PAN-ROASTED Eggplant
with Shallot Vinaigrette

Blistered ZUCCHINI Skillet
Gratin

Seared YELLOW WAX
BEANS 'N' GREENS

GROUPER *with* **Lemon-
Caper** Butter

TUNA STEAK **au Poivre**
with Cognac Sauce

Branzino *with* WHOLE
TOMATOES *and* **Basil**

SEARED SCALLOPS,
Shiitake Fricassee, *and*
GARLICKY Spinach

Killer GARLIC **Shrimp**

Chicken PROVENÇAL

CHICKEN THIGHS in White Wine and Herbs

Spicy CITRUS-GLAZED Duck Breasts

RICOTTA- and PANCETTA-Stuffed Pork Chops

BLACK and BLUE Beef Tenderloin

Tri-Tips with SALSA VERDE

PAN-ROASTED Eggplant with Shallot VINAIGRETTE

VINNY: Eggplant was our secret ingredient when we were on *Iron Chef*. This is a simplified version of the Italian eggplant dish called *caponata,* similar to what we made on that episode.

Jon: Being on *Iron Chef* was one of the coolest and most exciting food experiences of our lives. Even though we lost by one point, to us, a couple of kids from Florida, just getting on the show was a huge win.

SLICE the eggplants in half lengthwise. Season the cut sides with the salt and set aside.

Heat 2 tablespoons of the oil in a stainless skillet over medium-high heat until the oil is shimmering (but not smoking), 1 to 2 minutes. Add the eggplant cut side down and cook until browned, 4 to 5 minutes. Flip the eggplant and cook until the skin side is browned and the eggplant is cooked through, another 2 to 3 minutes. Transfer to a serving platter and set aside.

Pour the remaining 1 tablespoon of oil in the pan and add the shallots and garlic, cooking, stirring often, until the garlic is fragrant, about 1 minute. Turn off the heat and stir in the capers, lemon juice, balsamic vinegar, basil, parsley, and sugar. Add the butter, swirl to incorporate, and pour the sauce over the cut side of the eggplants.

SERVES 4

3 Italian or Japanese eggplants

1 teaspoon kosher salt

3 tablespoons canola or grapeseed oil

3 shallots, halved and thinly sliced

2 garlic cloves, thinly sliced

2 tablespoons drained capers

2 tablespoons fresh lemon juice

2 teaspoons balsamic vinegar

1 tablespoon finely chopped fresh basil

1½ teaspoons finely chopped fresh flat-leaf parsley

1½ teaspoons sugar

1 tablespoon unsalted butter

BLISTERED Zucchini SKILLET GRATIN

1 tablespoon olive oil
2 medium zucchini,
   sliced ⅛ inch thick
1 teaspoon kosher salt
½ lemon
½ cup finely grated
   Parmigiano-Reggiano
   cheese

If you don't have a stainless skillet that can go from stovetop to oven without a problem, then after sautéing the zucchini, transfer it to an oven-safe gratin dish and finish it off under the broiler. This dish also works nicely with butternut squash.

PREHEAT your broiler to high and set an oven rack at the upper-middle position.

Heat the oil in a skillet over high heat until the oil is shimmering, about 1 minute. Add the zucchini, season with the salt, and cook until browned, 2 to 3 minutes. Using tongs, flip each piece over and cook the other side until browned, another 2 to 3 minutes.

Turn off the heat, squeeze the lemon juice over the zucchini, and transfer to a large bowl. Sprinkle the cheese on top and serve.

SERVES 4

is it hot yet?

We recommend heating your skillet and oil together so they get hot at the same time (unless you're trying to get a really strong sear on a piece of meat or fish— then you want to heat the skillet for a couple of minutes before adding the oil). If you heat the pan first and then add the oil once the pan is already hot, you've got to be ready to move; that oil can get smoky right quick. You have a little more time if you heat the oil and the pan together. Once the oil gets a shimmer to it and grows "legs"—meaning it streaks across a hot skillet—you know it's hot enough to start cooking.

SEARED YELLOW
Wax BEANS 'N' GREENS

Jon: After sampling Jonathan Waxman's wax beans at Barbuto in New York City, we developed a newfound respect for this legume and how delicious it can be. It's a really seasonal dish, best made in the summer when wax beans are abundant.

VINNY: This dish is so simple and fresh. It's great warm or cold. We sometimes add thinly sliced fresh fennel for a little anisey flavor.

HEAT the oil and garlic in a stainless skillet over medium heat until the garlic begins to become fragrant, about 1 minute. Add the shallots and beans and stir often until they are nicely browned, about 5 minutes (if they get dark too quickly, reduce the heat to medium-low).

Stir in the thyme, red pepper flakes, salt, and then the lemon juice and cook until the beans are tender, 3 to 5 minutes. Stir in the arugula leaves, cooking until they are just wilted, about another 2 minutes. Serve hot, at room temperature, or cold.

SERVES 4

⅓ cup olive oil

3 garlic cloves, thinly sliced

3 shallots, thinly sliced

1 pound yellow wax beans, ends trimmed

1½ teaspoons finely chopped fresh thyme

½ teaspoon red pepper flakes

1½ teaspoons kosher salt

2 tablespoons fresh lemon juice

2 cups packed baby arugula leaves or larger arugula leaves, tough stems trimmed

GROUPER *with* Lemon-Caper BUTTER

4 6- to 8-ounce ¾- to 1-inch-thick skinless grouper fillets (see Note)

2 teaspoons kosher salt

4 tablespoons (½ stick) unsalted butter

¼ cup capers (rinsed if salt-packed; drained if brine-packed)

2 lemons, halved

2 teaspoons finely chopped fresh flat-leaf parsley

> **note**
> Can't find grouper? Substitute halibut. It will be a little flakier than the grouper and just as delicious.

If the butter goes from dark brown to black while the fish is cooking, then after plating the fish drain the dark butter off and add a fresh tablespoon of butter to the pan. It will melt quickly. Then proceed with sauce as described below.

SPRINKLE all sides of the fish fillets with the salt.

Melt 2 tablespoons of the butter in a stainless skillet over medium-high heat. Add the fish and sear until it is opaque halfway through, 4 to 5 minutes. Add the remaining 2 tablespoons of butter to the skillet and, once it has melted, flip the fillets and sear on the second side until completely cooked through and the fillets slightly resist semifirm pressure when pressed, another 3 to 4 minutes.

Transfer the fish to plates. Add the capers to the hot skillet and let them sizzle for 15 seconds (if they don't sizzle, place the skillet over medium-high heat for 30 seconds or until they start to sizzle). Squeeze the lemon juice over the capers, sprinkle with the parsley, and stir to combine. Drizzle the lemon-caper butter over the fillets and serve immediately.

SERVES 4

. . . VARIATION

SHRIMP WITH ANCHOVY-CAPER BUTTER

Substitute 2 pounds peeled and deveined shrimp for the grouper and cook them in 2 tablespoons unsalted butter over medium-high heat for about 2 minutes or until curled and opaque nearly all the way through. Add 2 finely chopped anchovy fillets to the pan along with the capers. Omit the lemon juice. Serve the sauce over the shrimp.

TUNA Steak au Poivre *with* COGNAC SAUCE

Take the flavor of your peppercorns to the next level by toasting them whole in a dry skillet for a few minutes before you crack them in your peppermill. Toasted peppercorns have an amazing spicy-smoky flavor that really works with the richness of tuna.

HEAT a stainless skillet over high heat for 2 minutes. Season the tuna steaks with the salt and then press pepper onto one side of each fillet. Add the oil and butter to your skillet, set the tuna steaks in the skillet pepper side down, and sear for 30 seconds without moving. Flip the tuna steaks over and sear the other side for another 30 seconds. Transfer the tuna to a plate and set aside.

To make the sauce, drain off any fat remaining in the skillet and reduce the heat to medium-high. Add 1 tablespoon of the butter. Once melted, add the shallots and cook, stirring often, until they are translucent, 2 to 3 minutes. Stir in the cognac, mustard, and Worcestershire sauce and cook over medium heat until the liquid reduces and becomes slightly thick, about 2 minutes. Stir in the cream and green peppercorns, then swirl in the remaining 2 tablespoons of butter. Once the butter is melted, serve the sauce over the steaks.

SERVES 4

4 1-inch-thick ahi or yellowtail tuna steaks
1 teaspoon kosher salt
1 tablespoon cracked black peppercorns (see headnote)
1 tablespoon canola or grapeseed oil
1 tablespoon unsalted butter

FOR THE COGNAC SAUCE

3 tablespoons unsalted butter
1 tablespoon finely chopped shallots
⅓ cup cognac
1½ teaspoons Dijon mustard
1 teaspoon Worcestershire sauce
½ cup heavy cream
1 tablespoon drained green peppercorns in brine

skillet-smashed peppercorns

Here is a down-and-dirty way to crack peppercorns. Place whole peppercorns in a skillet over medium-high heat and toast them until fragrant, about 3 minutes. Roll the bottom and edge of another skillet over the peppercorns, using pressure to crush and crack them. You can grind the toasted peppercorns in a spice grinder, too.

Branzino *with* WHOLE TOMATOES *and* Basil

4 6- to 8-ounce branzino
    fillets
1½ teaspoons kosher salt
1 tablespoon olive oil
1 garlic clove, thinly sliced
1 shallot, halved and thinly
    sliced
1 pint grape or cherry
    tomatoes
2 tablespoons unsalted butter
Juice of ½ lemon
5 fresh basil leaves, roughly
    torn

Jon: Branzino, which is sometimes called Mediterranean sea bass, is a really fantastic mellow-flavored and flaky white fish. Red snapper, sea bass, and trout all share the same mild-flavored and firm-textured characteristics and would work in this recipe.

VINNY: Sungolds and Sweet 100 tomatoes are intensely sweet and juicy varieties of cherry tomatoes. When we can get them, we'll use them in this recipe. If we can't find them, then we just use the best-quality small tomato—be it grape or cherry—that we can lay our hands on.

SEASON the fish with 1 teaspoon of the salt and set aside.

Heat a stainless skillet over medium-high heat for 2 minutes. Add the olive oil to the pan and then add the fish, skin side down. Place another smaller heavy skillet or pot (make sure the bottom of the pot is cool to the touch) on top of the fish to weight it down so it doesn't curl. (If your pan or pot isn't heavy enough, you can add rice or a couple of cans of beans or other canned items—still in the can!—to the pot to help add weight.) Cook until the skin is browned and crisp, 4 to 6 minutes. Flip the fillets and cook the other side until the fish is cooked through, another 3 to 5 minutes.

Transfer the fish to a platter or individual plates and set aside. Add the garlic and shallots to the skillet and cook, stirring often, until the garlic is fragrant, about 1 minute. Add the tomatoes, season with the remaining ½ teaspoon of salt, and cook until their skins start to split and the juices begin to run. Swirl in the butter and lemon juice, then stir in the basil and pour over the fish.

SERVES 4

SEARED SCALLOPS, Shiitake Fricassee, *and* GARLICKY SPINACH

2 tablespoons plus
    2 teaspoons canola
    or grapeseed oil
6 ounces shiitake
    mushrooms, stems
    removed, caps thinly
    sliced
2 teaspoons kosher salt
4 garlic cloves, thinly sliced
6 cups packed spinach, tough
    stems removed
2 tablespoons unsalted butter
2 shallots, very finely
    chopped
1 teaspoon finely chopped
    fresh thyme
2 tablespoons fresh lemon
    juice
16 "dry" sea scallops
    (see Note, opposite)

Jon: This recipe right here is the one that gave us the idea for this book; it's really how we used to cook when we were starting out. We would literally cook everything off in one pan because that's all we had. It taught us how to manage our time and make our recipes concise.

VINNY: By producing three completely separate components for a dish in one pan, we learned how to work through the procedure, steps, and order of preparation for making this kind of one-pan cooking work. It forces you to approach cooking from a strategic viewpoint.

HEAT 1 tablespoon of the oil in a stainless skillet over medium-high heat for 1 minute. Add the mushrooms, season with 1 teaspoon of the salt, and cook until browned, 6 to 8 minutes, stirring occasionally. Transfer to a small bowl, cover with plastic wrap to keep warm, and set aside.

Add 2 teaspoons of the oil the pan and then add half of the garlic, sautéing it until it is fragrant, about 1 minute. Add the spinach and ½ teaspoon of the salt and cook until wilted but still bright green, 1 to 2 minutes. Transfer to a small bowl, cover with plastic wrap to keep warm, and set aside.

Melt the butter in the skillet, then add the shallots and the remaining garlic. Cook until the garlic is golden brown and the butter is beginning to brown, about 2 minutes. Turn off the heat and stir in the thyme, lemon juice, and the reserved mushrooms. Transfer the mixture back to the small bowl, re-cover, and set aside.

Use paper towels to wipe out the pan. Heat the remaining 1 tablespoon of oil over high heat in the skillet for 1 minute. Season the scallops with the remaining ½ teaspoon of salt and place them in the pan. Sear the scallops without moving until golden brown, about 2 minutes. Flip the scallops over and cook until the other side has color (it probably won't get as dark as the first side) and the scallops are opaque on the outside and still a little translucent in the center (slice one in half to check), another 30 seconds to 1 minute.

Divide the scallops among 4 plates. Spoon some of the mushroom fricassee on top of each and serve the spinach on the side.

SERVES 4

what's a "dry" scallop?

Get ready for this: most scallops in your grocery store are dipped in sodium tripolyphosphate (STP), which helps scallops retain moisture so they can stay on the shelf longer. These are called "wet" scallops. "Dry" scallops, on the other hand, have no preservatives and a water content of less than 80 percent; because they're dryer, they take on a nicer sear in a hot pan. When buying scallops, you know that they've been dipped in STP if they're pure white; dry scallops have a natural peachy-brown tint. If you're lucky enough to find dry diver scallops, buy them; they are hand-harvested by divers and are usually very fresh.

KILLER GARLIC Shrimp

2 pounds extra-large
    (10 to 15 per pound)
    shrimp, peeled and
    deveined
10 garlic cloves, finely
    chopped
¼ cup olive oil
2 teaspoons kosher salt
Pinch of red pepper flakes
¼ cup chopped fresh cilantro
4 limes, cut into wedges

Jon: We only use extra-virgin olive oil for finishing a dish once it's ready to serve. It has a low smoking point, so you can't cook with it at high temperatures—not to mention that it's expensive.

VINNY: Plus, its delicate flavors are killed when the oil gets hot. When it comes down to it, though, if it's all we've got in the kitchen, we'll use it. Otherwise we cook with grapeseed or canola oil, or our house blend of 80 percent grapeseed/canola mixed with 20 percent extra-virgin olive oil.

PLACE the shrimp in a large bowl and toss with the garlic and oil. Cover with plastic wrap and refrigerate for 30 minutes or up to 1 hour.

Heat a stainless skillet over medium-high heat for 2 minutes. Add the salt to the shrimp and toss to combine, then add the shrimp and the marinade to the hot skillet. Cook until the shrimp are curled and slightly firm to the touch, 2 to 3 minutes, stirring often.

Transfer the shrimp to a serving bowl and sprinkle with a pinch of red pepper flakes and the cilantro. Serve immediately, with the limes on the side.

SERVES 4

Chicken PROVENÇAL

The bold taste of olives and capers rocks this dish out. If you prefer boneless chicken breasts to bone-in breasts, feel free to substitute them, but reduce the cooking time, since boneless breasts cook faster. If you can't find butter beans, use any white bean, such as cannellini, Great Northern, or navy beans. Serve with a few wedges of rustic bread to sop up all of the sauce.

PLACE the flour in a shallow dish. Season the chicken with ½ teaspoon of the salt and then dredge through the flour to lightly coat each side, tapping off any excess.

Heat a stainless skillet over medium-high heat for 2 minutes. Add ¼ cup of the oil to the skillet and when it's hot (after about 1 minute) sear the floured breasts skin side down until golden brown and crisp, 4 to 6 minutes. (If the skin gets too dark too quickly, reduce the heat to medium.) Sear the chicken in two batches if your pan isn't big enough. Flip the breasts over and sear the other side until browned, another 4 to 6 minutes. Transfer the chicken to a plate and set aside.

Drain off all of the fat in the pan. Place the skillet back over medium-high heat and add 3 tablespoons of the butter. Once melted, add the garlic and cook until it is fragrant, 30 seconds to 1 minute. Add the wine, tomatoes, olives, anchovy paste, and the remaining ½ teaspoon of salt and cook, stirring often, until the sauce thickens, 4 to 5 minutes.

Add the beans and the remaining 3 tablespoons of butter and once it is melted, return the chicken to the pan, skin side up, along with any accumulated juices. Simmer until the chicken is completely cooked through, 8 to 12 minutes.

Place the chicken on individual plates. Stir the basil into the sauce and pour over the chicken. Serve immediately.

SERVES 4

½ cup all-purpose flour
4 6- to 8-ounce bone-in chicken breasts, with skin
1 teaspoon kosher salt
¾ cup canola or grapeseed oil
6 tablespoons (¾ stick) unsalted butter
2 garlic cloves, thinly sliced
½ cup plus 2 tablespoons dry white wine (such as pinot grigio or sauvignon blanc)
3 large tomatoes, halved, seeded, and finely chopped
½ cup pitted and roughly chopped green olives (we like French Lucques olives for this)
1 anchovy fillet, finely chopped to a paste
1 15-ounce can butter beans, drained and rinsed
6 large fresh basil leaves, roughly torn

CHICKEN THIGHS *in* White Wine *and* HERBS

8 skin-on boneless chicken thighs

2 teaspoons kosher salt

1½ teaspoons canola or grapeseed oil

2 shallots, thinly sliced

1½ tablespoons sherry vinegar

⅔ cup dry white wine (such as pinot grigio or sauvignon blanc)

1½ teaspoons finely chopped fresh marjoram

1½ teaspoons finely chopped fresh flat-leaf parsley

1 teaspoon finely chopped fresh thyme

2 tablespoons unsalted butter

VINNY: This is the kind of dish we used to make as staff meals in restaurants: it's quick, comforting, and really delicious. Staff meals are one of the best perks of our jobs!

Jon: Chicken thighs are so underutilized. Sure, you could use chicken breasts in this recipe if you prefer, but thighs have so much more flavor, plus, you don't have to worry about them drying out like you do a chicken breast.

SEASON the chicken with 1½ teaspoons of salt and set aside.

Heat the oil in a large stainless skillet over medium-high heat until the oil shimmers, 1 to 2 minutes. Place half of the chicken in the pan, skin side down, and cook until it is golden brown, 8 to 10 minutes. Flip the thighs and cook until the other side is browned, the chicken is cooked through, and the juices run clear (not pink), another 10 minutes. Repeat with the remaining chicken, scraping any browned bits from the bottom of the pan between batches (if you can't scrape them up that's okay; they'll come up after you add the vinegar, below).

Transfer the chicken to a large platter and set aside. Pour off all but 1 tablespoon of the fat left in the pan and discard.

Add the shallots to the skillet and cook, stirring often, until they are beginning to soften, 2 to 3 minutes. Add the vinegar and simmer for 1 minute while scraping and stirring up any browned bits from the bottom of the pan. Add ⅓ cup water and the wine and cook until the amount of liquid left in the skillet is about ⅓ cup, 7 to 8 minutes. Stir in the herbs, butter, and remaining ½ teaspoon of salt, pour over the chicken, and serve.

SERVES 4

SPICY Citrus-Glazed DUCK BREASTS

FOR THE GLAZE

1 cup fresh orange juice
   (from about 4 oranges)
Juice of 1 lemon
¼ cup rice vinegar
1 tablespoon soy sauce
1 tablespoon fresh lime juice
1 tablespoon honey
½ fennel bulb, cored and
   finely chopped, a few
   fronds reserved for garnish
2 shallots, halved and thinly
   sliced
1 jalapeño or serrano chile,
   seeded and finely chopped
2 whole star anise
2 tablespoons sugar
2 tablespoons unsalted butter

FOR THE DUCK

4 8-ounce skin-on boneless
   duck breasts
1½ teaspoons kosher salt
1 teaspoon canola or
   grapeseed oil

We like this salty-sweet duck dish with simple sides, such as plain white rice, fried rice, some green beans, or Scallion Pancakes (see below).

WHISK together all of the glaze ingredients, except for the butter, in a medium bowl and set aside.

Score the duck skin on the diagonal in ½-inch intervals, and again in the opposite direction so it is marked with a diamond pattern. Season the meat with the salt.

Heat a large stainless skillet over medium-high heat for 2 minutes. Add the oil and place the duck breasts, skin side down, in the pan. Reduce the heat to medium-high and cook until the skin is browned and crisp, 5 to 7 minutes. Turn the duck breasts and cook the second side until browned, 2 to 3 minutes; transfer the duck to a plate and cover with aluminum foil to keep warm. Drain off all but 2 tablespoons of the fat in the pan.

Add the glaze mixture to the skillet and cook over medium-high heat until the liquid is thick and syrupy, 8 to 10 minutes. Swirl in the remaining butter, then return the duck breasts to the skillet, turning to coat in the glaze. Serve immediately.

SERVES 4

+1 pan: scallion pancakes

Follow our pancake recipe on page 62, substituting whole milk for the buttermilk. Add 8 trimmed and thinly sliced scallions (white and light green parts only) to the batter, and ladle the batter in ¼-cup increments onto an electric griddle, a stovetop griddle, or a nonstick pan. One recipe will make about 12 scallion pancakes.

RICOTTA- *and* PANCETTA-STUFFED Pork Chops

4 1½- to 2-inch-thick pork
    rib chops
2 tablespoons canola or
    grapeseed oil (plus more if
    necessary)
1 medium yellow onion,
    finely chopped
8 ⅛- to ¼-inch-thick
    pancetta slices, chopped
    into ½-inch squares
1 cup fresh ricotta cheese
1 teaspoon finely chopped
    fresh thyme
1 teaspoon kosher salt
2 cups Classic Marinara
    (page 120)
1 tablespoon finely chopped
    fresh flat-leaf parsley

VINNY: Salt encourages onions to release water—which is not a good thing if you're trying to brown and caramelize onions! To get that sticky, supple sweetness that makes caramelized onions so good, it's important to hold back the salt until the very end so the sugars get a chance to brown.

Jon: Though I'm lactose intolerant, I'll absolutely punish myself to eat this dish! The taste of the pork chops with the ricotta is so amazing. Set aside a little of the sauce and toss it with some al dente pasta or fried eggplant for a full-on comfort meal.

PREHEAT your oven to 500°F. Make a long and deep slit about ½ inch from the bone in the meaty edge of each pork chop. Use the tip of your knife to tunnel into the center of the meat, making a pocket for the stuffing. Set the chops aside.

Heat a stainless skillet over medium-high heat for 2 minutes. Add the oil and the onions and cook for 2 to 3 minutes, stirring often. Reduce the heat to medium-low and cook the onions until soft and sticky, another 8 to 10 minutes, stirring often. Transfer the onions to a plate and set aside. Add the pancetta to the hot skillet and cook until all sides are crisp and browned, 5 to 8 minutes. Turn off the heat and transfer the pancetta to a plate. Set aside to cool, leaving the fat from the pancetta in the pan.

Place the ricotta and thyme in a medium bowl.

Stir the cooled pancetta, caramelized onions, and ½ teaspoon of the salt into the ricotta until well blended. Stuff some of the mixture into each pork chop, stuffing the pocket so it is full but not spilling out.

Heat your skillet over medium-high heat for 2 minutes and season both sides of the pork chops with the remaining ½ teaspoon of salt. Add the pork chops to the skillet and sear until crispy and golden brown on both sides, 8 to 10 minutes total. Transfer the chops to a plate and drain off the fat in the skillet. Return the chops to the skillet and cover with the marinara sauce. Transfer the entire skillet to the oven and bake until the sauce is bubbly and the chops are completely cooked through, about 15 minutes. Sprinkle with the parsley and serve immediately.

SERVES 4

CLASSIC MARINARA

2 28-ounce cans whole
   tomatoes packed in juice
   (not purée)
⅓ cup olive oil
20 garlic cloves, thinly sliced
1 teaspoon red pepper flakes
1 tablespoon kosher salt
20 whole fresh basil leaves

This is our straight-up recipe for classic marinara sauce. Make a double batch and freeze whatever is left over in smaller portions. It'll come in handy for saucing pan-seared pork chops, chicken breasts, pasta and ravioli, and even pizza.

Place the tomatoes and their juices in a large bowl. Using your hands, squeeze and shred the tomatoes into small bits.

Heat the oil and garlic in a soup pot over medium heat just until the garlic begins to toast, 7 to 9 minutes. Add the red pepper flakes and then stir in the tomatoes and salt. Cook until slightly thickened and the sauce has darkened, about 45 minutes, then stir in the basil. Taste for seasoning.

MAKES 6 CUPS

BLACK *and* BLUE BEEF TENDERLOIN

VINNY: It's important to recognize the classics, and the brandy cream sauce on these steaks is one of them. We served steak this way for a client who was having a 1970s-themed party. It was such a hit that we started serving it more often. Also called a "Diane" sauce, it is a great example of a simple and delicious sauce that deserves to make a comeback.

Jon: You've got to make sure that your skillet gets really hot for this one. You want the steak to be extremely seared on the outside and nearly raw within. If you want your black and blue not *so* blue in the middle, though, lower the heat on the pan and let the steak sear a little longer.

HEAT a skillet over high heat for 3 minutes. Sprinkle the steaks with the salt, add the oil to the skillet, and sear until both sides are deeply browned and nearly charred, 2 to 3 minutes per side for a very rare center. (If you want your steaks less rare in the middle, reduce the heat to medium-high after turning them and continue cooking until the steaks are cooked to your preference.) Transfer the steaks to a platter or individual plates, cover with aluminum foil to keep warm, and set aside.

Drain off any fat from the skillet. Melt 2 tablespoons of the butter over medium-high heat. Once melted, add the mushrooms, shallots, garlic, and salt and cook until the mushrooms are soft, 2 to 4 minutes. Add the brandy and cook for 1 minute, then add the cream, lemon juice, Worcestershire sauce, mustard, and thyme. Cook until the sauce is thick, 3 to 4 minutes, stirring often. Stir in the remaining table-spoon of butter, the parsley, and chives (if using). Once the butter is incorporated, taste for seasoning, and pour the sauce over the steaks. Serve immediately.

SERVES 4

FOR THE STEAKS

4 6- to 8-ounce filet mignons or 1 1½- to 2-pound beef tenderloin cut in 4 pieces
½ teaspoon kosher salt
1½ tablespoons canola or grapeseed oil

FOR THE SAUCE

3 tablespoons unsalted butter
2 ounces white button or cremini mushroom caps, thinly sliced (about 1 cup)
1 large shallot, finely diced
1 garlic clove, thinly sliced
½ teaspoon kosher salt
¼ cup plus 2 tablespoons brandy
½ cup heavy cream
1 tablespoon fresh lemon juice
2 teaspoons Worcestershire sauce
1½ teaspoons Dijon mustard
½ teaspoon finely chopped fresh thyme
2 teaspoons finely chopped fresh flat-leaf parsley
2 teaspoons finely chopped fresh chives (optional)

TRI-TIPS *with* Salsa Verde

FOR THE SALSA VERDE

⅓ cup extra-virgin olive oil

Juice and grated zest of
    1 lemon

2 anchovy fillets, very finely
    chopped

2 garlic cloves, very finely
    chopped

1 tablespoon drained capers,
    roughly chopped

1 tablespoon finely chopped
    fresh oregano

1 tablespoon finely chopped
    fresh flat-leaf parsley

1 teaspoon finely chopped
    fresh mint

½ teaspoon kosher salt

FOR THE STEAK

2 1½-pound tri-tip steaks,
    sliced crosswise into
    1¼-inch-thick planks

1 teaspoon kosher salt

1½ teaspoons grapeseed oil

VINNY: A lot of different countries do up a salsa verde. Ours is closest to the Italian version. It's got this amazing salty green flavor, and it is excellent with steak, chicken, and lamb. Though it keeps for up to one day, the herbs will become less potent the longer it sits.

Jon: The tri-tip steak is a California original whose origins go back more than one hundred years to the central coast, where it was barbecued over red oak wood. It is now synonymous with Santa Maria–style barbecue. Outside of California, it's a somewhat overlooked cut (see Note) that deserves to be discovered.

PLACE the salsa verde ingredients in a medium bowl and whisk together to combine. (The salsa verde can be made up to 1 day ahead.)

Season the steak with the salt and set aside. Heat a large stainless skillet over medium-high heat for 2 minutes. Add the oil to the pan and when it is hot, sear the steak until it is browned, 3 to 5 minutes. Flip the steak and cook the other side until browned, about another 3 to 5 minutes for rare, or 5 to 6 minutes for medium-rare to medium (use a knife to cut into the steak to check the interior color for doneness). Serve with salsa verde spooned over the top.

SERVES 6

---

name game

Tri-tip comes from the loin, and while it is not as tender as other loin cuts, such as filet mignon, nor as famous as the T-bone, it has a nice, beefy flavor and great price point that make it a solid cut worth knowing about. In the West you see a lot of tri-tips; in other parts of the country tri-tip steaks might be labeled as a sirloin tip or loin tip. Flank steak (sometimes called London broil), another strongly grained muscle, is a good substitute.

DUTCH OVEN

Jon: When we were living in Colorado and working at the Lodge at Vail's Wildflower restaurant, we'd throw a pot of meat in the oven on our days off and come back after a few hours of snowboarding with a massive appetite. The whole house would be filled with the most amazing smells. We'd pull the pot out of the oven and totally dig into some oxtails or osso buco! That's where our love for low-and-slow cooking first began.

VINNY: This is actually my favorite kind of cooking. It's simple, but made with a lot of love. You can create truly beautiful meals with just a few ingredients and some time. It's like life: great things happen with time.

Jon: Watch out, here comes the philosopher.

VINNY: Well, it's easy, too. You put it in the oven and forget about it. Wait, scratch that. Don't forget about it! Just focus your attention somewhere else while it's in the oven. Make a killer dessert, or read a book or something.

Jon: Because these dishes are cooked wet, rather than dry (as in roasting), they're very forgiving. You could innocently overcook them a little, and they'd still be great—even the vegetables. The liquid keeps the meat moist and tender and gives it that pull-off-the-bone quality.

VINNY: The vegetables that we chose to include in this chapter, like artichokes, escarole, and long beans, all benefit from extra tenderness, too.

Jon: Yeah—there's nothing wrong with serving melt-in-your-mouth tender vegetables. Not everything has to be al dente all the time!

VINNY: With the artichokes being the exception, you never want the ingredients to be fully submerged in the liquid. I always like it when a little peeks out at the top. That part gets a nice, crusty quality that is a good contrast to the buttery meat.

Jon: Most of these dishes are economical, too, since they are made with inexpensive cuts of meat that need a long time in the oven to get tender. They're great choices for all you starving artists out there.

VINNY: We also save money and time by skipping the stock. Traditionally, these recipes were made with a rich stock, but we don't have the refrigerator or freezer space or the time to devote to making real stock. So we've figured out ways to introduce deep flavors without it, using ingredients such as beer, pancetta, wine, and ketchup to build flavor instead.

Jon: What it comes down to is this: when you're in trouble—with your parents, your roommate, or your significant other—pull out a pot of lamb shanks or duck quarters from the oven and see just how quickly they forget whatever was on their mind.

MENU

OLIVE OIL–BRAISED Baby Artichokes

Blank Canvas MASHED POTATOES

Garlic-Braised *Brothy* **ESCAROLE**

Garlicky **Long BEANS**

CREAMED BRUSSELS SPROUTS *with* **Bacon**

Asparagus RISOTTO

FRANK'S Clam Chowder

White Wine *and* **Tarragon STEAMED MUSSELS**

LOBSTER Rolls

Beer-Battered Cod *and* **TARTAR SAUCE**

Duck Quarters *with* **DRIED FRUIT** *and* **Sherry**

Amatriciana-Style CHICKEN LEGS *and* **Thighs**

BUTTERMILK-SAGE Fried Chicken

BUCATINI CARBONARA, Pancetta, *and* **Peas**

Slow-Cooked LAMB SHANKS *in* Pinot Noir

White Wine–Braised **OSSO BUCO**

VINNY'S Spaghetti Bolognese

BEER-BRAISED SHORT RIBS *and* **Shiitakes**

"BIG RED" *with* **Brisket** *and* Pinto Beans

OLIVE OIL–BRAISED BABY Artichokes

2 lemons, halved
20 fresh baby artichokes
   (about 1¾ pounds)
2 quarts olive oil (see Tip)
1 teaspoon kosher salt
¼ teaspoon freshly ground
   black pepper
1 2-ounce chunk Parmigiano-
   Reggiano cheese, shaved
   into ribbons with a
   vegetable peeler

tip

After removing the vegetables, strain the oil through a fine-mesh sieve to remove any debris and save the olive oil for another use, such as making frittatas, French fries, or a vinaigrette. You don't need to use expensive extra-virgin olive oil here; use cooking olive oil. To save money, you can even use 2 cups canola oil to 6 cups olive oil.

VINNY: Lots of things, including fennel, new potatoes, and even tuna, are delicious slow-poached in olive oil. But our faves are artichokes.

Jon: Oil and water don't mix, so be sure to drain the artichokes really well before poaching.

PREHEAT your oven to 300°F.

Fill a large bowl with cold water. Squeeze the juice of 2 lemon halves into the water, add the squeezed rinds, and set aside. Rinse the artichokes under cold water and then use a vegetable peeler to peel away the fibrous outer layer of the stems. Pull off the tough outer leaves, slice ¼ to ½ inch off of the top of each artichoke, and slice off the very end of the stem to get a clean cut. Place the trimmed artichokes in the lemon water as you go so they don't discolor.

Once they are all cleaned, drain the artichokes, shaking the colander to remove as much water as possible. Turn the artichokes out onto a clean kitchen towel for a couple of minutes to drain completely.

Place the artichokes in a Dutch oven, and pour enough olive oil over them to cover completely by ½ inch. Cover the pot, and bake until a paring knife slips easily into the center of an artichoke, about 45 minutes.

Let the artichokes stand in the oil until cooled to room temperature, about 1½ hours. Use a slotted spoon to transfer the artichokes to a serving dish, sprinkle with the salt and pepper, and drizzle with a little of the cooking oil. Squeeze the remaining lemon halves over the artichokes, finish them with the shaved cheese, and serve.

SERVES 4 TO 6

BLANK CANVAS
Mashed POTATOES

These mashed potatoes are the perfect base for so many flavors. You could add goat cheese, lobster, root vegetable purée, bacon, chives, Cheddar, or mozzarella. Or serve them straight up; they're nice and creamy, because we use lots of butter and cream.

FILL a Dutch oven with water and bring to a boil. Add the 2 tablespoons of salt and the potatoes and cook until the potatoes are fork-tender, about 15 to 18 minutes. Drain and set aside.

Combine the butter and cream in the pot and heat to a simmer, stirring until the butter is melted. Return the potatoes to the pot and mash with a sturdy whisk or with a potato masher (don't stir the potatoes too much, otherwise they'll get gluey). Season with salt if necessary and serve.

SERVES 10 TO 12

2 tablespoons kosher salt, plus extra for seasoning
5 pounds russet potatoes, peeled, halved lengthwise, and each half quartered
1 cup (2 sticks) unsalted butter
1½ cups heavy cream

---

keeping mashed potatoes warm and reheating

If you have to make your mashed potatoes ahead of time, keep them warm in a large, wide bowl set over a large pot with an inch or two of barely simmering water in it (the bottom of the bowl shouldn't touch the water). Cover with plastic wrap and stir just before serving. When reheating cold mashed potatoes, add a tablespoon or two of extra cream and butter, then microwave for a couple of minutes on high, stirring once. Mashed potatoes get starchy and dry, so adding a bit more hot cream and melted butter gets them creamy again.

Garlic-Braised BROTHY ESCAROLE

1 tablespoon olive oil

6 garlic cloves, thinly sliced

2 large or 3 medium heads of escarole, leaves separated, washed, and sliced cross-wise into 1-inch-wide strips

3 tablespoons unsalted butter

1½ teaspoons kosher salt

VINNY: Escarole is an underused leafy green. It's sturdy enough to braise, and mild enough to please lots of people who don't get into more bitter braised greens. For a meal-in-one dish, add some cooked pasta and white beans.

Jon: My favorite way to eat this is in a bowl with a nice steak on the side. Be sure to dip pieces of the steak in the sauce to soak up all that garlicky goodness.

HEAT the olive oil in a Dutch oven over medium-high heat. Add the garlic and cook until fragrant, stirring, about 1 minute. Stir in the escarole and cook until slightly wilted, about 1 minute. Add 1½ cups water, bring to a simmer, and cook until the escarole is tender, 7 to 9 minutes. Add the butter and salt and, once the butter has melted, serve.

SERVES 6

GARLICKY Long Beans

2 tablespoons plus 1 teaspoon kosher salt

3 pounds green beans, ends trimmed

8 tablespoons (1 stick) unsalted butter

12 garlic cloves

These green beans are tender and comforting, kind of like your grandma might have made. We cook them just long enough to get soft without falling apart.

FILL a Dutch oven with water and bring to a boil. Add the 2 tablespoons of salt and the green beans and cook until the beans are quite tender but still have body, 6 to 9 minutes. Drain the beans and place under cold running water to stop the cooking. Drain again and set aside.

Place the pot back over medium heat. Add the butter and, once melted, add the garlic and cook for 2 minutes. Add the green beans and cook until they are warmed through, 3 to 5 minutes. Add 1 teaspoon salt, toss, and serve.

SERVES 8

CREAMED Brussels Sprouts *with* BACON

Jon: A lot of people who say that they don't do Brussels sprouts end up getting into this dish. Cream and bacon mellow Brussels sprouts' cabbagey qualities.

VINNY: We add so much bacon, butter, and cream, though, you'd have to be insane not to totally get into this dish! We get a lot of requests for these Brussels sprouts around Thanksgiving. There are a few families whose Thanksgiving dinners we've been catering for years; we've become a part of their tradition. That's really cool.

FILL a Dutch oven with water and bring to a boil. Add the 1 tablespoon of salt and the Brussels sprouts. Cook until tender but not mushy, 5 to 7 minutes. Drain the sprouts, then place them under cold running water to stop the cooking. Drain again, transfer the sprouts to a cutting board, and halve lengthwise. Set aside.

Wipe the pot dry and place it back on the stovetop over medium-high heat. Add the bacon (if it doesn't all fit in the pot, cook the bacon in two batches) and cook until both sides are browned and crisp. Transfer to a paper-towel-lined plate to drain. Once it is cool enough to handle, crumble the bacon.

Pour off all but 1 tablespoon of the bacon fat and add the shallots and garlic to the pot. Cook over medium-high heat until lightly browned and fragrant, about 2 minutes, and then add the cream. Simmer the cream until it has reduced by half, 5 to 7 minutes, and add the remaining 1 teaspoon of salt and the black pepper. Stir in the Brussels sprouts and gently coat in the sauce. Turn out into a serving bowl and top with the crumbled bacon.

SERVES 6 TO 8

1 tablespoon plus 1 teaspoon kosher salt

2 pounds Brussels sprouts, outer leaves removed

12 ounces sliced bacon, halved crosswise

2 shallots, halved and thinly sliced

3 garlic cloves, thinly sliced

3 cups heavy cream

1 teaspoon freshly ground black pepper

ASPARAGUS Risotto

4 tablespoons (½ stick)
   unsalted butter

½ shallot, very finely
   chopped

1 cup Arborio rice

½ cup dry white wine

2½ cups boiling water

12 ounces thin asparagus
   (about 1 bunch), ends
   trimmed, tips reserved,
   stalks sliced ⅛ inch thick

3 tablespoons mascarpone
   cheese

½ cup finely grated
   Parmigiano-Reggiano
   cheese

2 teaspoons kosher salt

Jon: There are two keys to great risotto: toasting the raw rice until it is opaque, and making sure that the liquid you add to the pot is really hot—and even boiling—before stirring it into the rice. Used in tandem, these tips ensure that your risotto will be al dente, not mushy. Since this is a delicately flavored risotto, we like to use water instead of chicken broth or vegetable stock. We find that you really experience the pure flavors of the asparagus and Parm this way.

VINNY: Here we leave the tender asparagus tips whole and slice the stalks really thin; the heat from the risotto is enough to cook the asparagus. The contrast between the creamy risotto, the just-cooked-through thin slices of asparagus, and the still-crunchy asparagus tips is really nice. Add some fresh peas for a quintessential springtime dish.

MELT 2 tablespoons of the butter in a Dutch oven over medium-high heat. Add the shallots and cook, stirring often, until they are soft, 2 to 3 minutes. Add the rice and cook, stirring often, until the grains are opaque, about 2 minutes. Stir in the wine and cook until it is completely absorbed, 2 to 3 minutes.

Add ¾ cup of the boiling water to the pot and stir the mixture constantly until it is completely absorbed into the rice. Add the remaining water in two additions, stirring constantly between additions and waiting until all of the water is absorbed before adding the next. The end texture should be somewhat al dente and very creamy, not pasty or gluey. It will take about 18 to 22 minutes from start to finish.

Stir in the asparagus, mascarpone, Parmigiano, remaining 2 tablespoons butter, and salt, and serve immediately.

SERVES 4 TO 6

SOUP POT

VINNY: I've never been in any kitchen—restaurant or home—that doesn't have a soup pot. If you only had one pot or pan in the house, a soup pot really could be it.

Jon: A soup pot opens the door to lots of options. Not all pots do that. Just because it's called a soup pot doesn't mean the only thing you can do with it is make soup!

VINNY: You can fry fish in it, poach lobster, cook vegetables, make chowders, and boil up pasta in it. Lots of stovetop dishes we make in the Dutch oven, such as mashed potatoes, mussels, chowder, and Bolognese sauce, can be made in a soup pot just as easily as in a Dutch oven.

Jon: In fact, you could adapt any of the recipes from our Dutch oven chapter to cook entirely on the stovetop in a soup pot.

VINNY: Quality-wise, you should get at least a six-quart heavy-gauge, thick-bottomed soup pot for making long-cooked items such as meat sauces. You can use a cheaper one for blanching vegetables or boiling, but if you're going to use your soup pot to get color on food before you add liquid, a pot with a solid structure will be better at conducting and retaining even heat.

Recipes that could also be made in a soup pot include:
- Blank Canvas Mashed Potatoes, page 133
- Garlic-Braised Brothy Escarole, page 134
- Garlicky Long Beans, page 134
- Creamed Brussels Sprouts with Bacon, page 137
- White Wine and Tarragon Steamed Mussels, page 144
- Frank's Clam Chowder, page 143
- Beer-Battered Cod and Tartar Sauce, page 148
- Lobster Rolls, page 147
- Bucatini Carbonara, Pancetta, and Peas, page 154
- Vinny's Spaghetti Bolognese, page 160
- "Big Red" with Brisket and Pinto Beans, page 165

FRANK'S CLAM CHOWDER

Our right-hand guy in the kitchen, Frank, is an important person in our lives. He has worked with us for years and really gets our style and our food. Frank is from Maine and his grandma taught him how to make this chowder. Trust us, it's killer. We like it with the Jonny 'Cakes on page 64.

MELT the butter in a Dutch oven over medium heat. Whisk in the flour and cook, while stirring, until it begins to bubble, about 2 minutes. Scrape the mixture (known as a *roux*) into a small bowl and set aside.

Use paper towels to wipe out the pot, and place it over medium-high heat. Add the bacon and cook until both sides are browned and crisp, 8 to 10 minutes. Transfer the bacon to a paper-towel-lined plate to drain. Once cool, crumble and set aside.

Add the potatoes to the bacon fat in the pot and cook, stirring often, until they begin to turn translucent around the edges, about 2 minutes. Stir in the carrots, celery, and onion. Cook, stirring often, until the potatoes start to brown, about another 4 minutes. Pour in the clam juice and add the chopped thyme and simmer until the broth is reduced by half, 4 to 6 minutes.

Pour in the cream and milk and bring to a boil. Simmer until the carrots are tender, 10 to 15 minutes, and then slowly stir in the roux a little at a time until the chowder is thick and hearty. Stir in the clams with their juices and the bacon, cook for 1 to 2 minutes to heat through, stir in the salt, and serve.

SERVES 8

4 tablespoons (½ stick) unsalted butter

⅓ cup all-purpose flour

8 ounces sliced bacon

2 medium russet potatoes, peeled and very finely chopped

2 medium carrots, peeled and finely chopped

2 celery stalks, finely chopped

1 onion, finely chopped

½ cup bottled clam juice

1½ teaspoons finely chopped fresh thyme

3 cups heavy cream

1 cup whole milk

1 6.5-ounce can of clams with their juices, roughly chopped

1 teaspoon kosher salt

White Wine *and* TARRAGON STEAMED Mussels

1 tablespoon olive oil

2 shallots, halved and thinly sliced

3 garlic cloves, thinly sliced

1 cup dry white wine (such as pinot grigio or sauvignon blanc)

½ teaspoon red pepper flakes

1 teaspoon kosher salt, plus extra for the bread

3 pounds mussels, debearded, scrubbed, and thoroughly rinsed (any open mussels discarded)

2 cups heavy cream

1 loaf of rustic bread, sliced

2 tablespoons olive oil

1 bunch of fresh chives, very finely chopped

2½ tablespoons roughly chopped fresh tarragon

This one-pot meal is really easy to put together for dinner, especially if you swing by your favorite fry joint on the way home and pick up some French fries to dip into the broth!

HEAT the oil in a Dutch oven over medium-high heat. Add the shallots and garlic and cook until they are just beginning to brown, about 2 minutes. Pour in the wine, scraping any browned bits off of the bottom of the pot, and stir in the red pepper flakes and the 1 teaspoon of salt.

Add the mussels to the pot, cover, and steam the mussels until they are just beginning to open, about 3 minutes. Pour in the cream, cover the pot again, and cook until all of the mussels are open, another 3 to 5 minutes (discard any mussels that don't open).

Meanwhile, brush the bread with olive oil and sprinkle with some salt. Broil or grill for a few minutes so one side is toasted. Remove the cover from the mussels, and turn them out into a large serving bowl or divide among individual bowls. Sprinkle with the chives and tarragon, and serve with the bread.

SERVES 6

tip

It's important to make sure all of your mussels are alive before you start cooking them. When you get home from the store, check to see they're all completely closed. If any are open, give them a tap. If the mussel closes up, it's fine. If it stays open, toss it.

you need to trim that beard, son

Cleaning mussels is really easy. Rinse them under cold water and discard any with broken shells. The "beard" is a hairy thread that hangs out around the tip of the mussel. Use your fingers to pull it off. After cooking, if there are any mussels that don't open, pitch them.

LOBSTER Rolls

Jon: There is something about warm buttered bread and cold lobster salad that is so completely awesome!

VINNY: I could eat five of these in a row!

PLACE the tip of a chef's knife at the X where the lobster head meets the body. Using a quick, strong motion, force the tip of the knife into the center of the X and slice down through the lobster's head and between its eyes (though the lobster's legs may still be moving, the lobster is dead). Twist the tail off of the body (save the body to make lobster stock if you like) and twist off the claws.

Fill a Dutch oven with water and bring to a near boil (the water should be at about 170°F). Add the ¼ cup of salt and the lobster claws. Cook the claws for 2 minutes, and then add the tails and cook for an additional 7 to 9 minutes (7 minutes for 1½-pound lobsters; 9 minutes for 2-pound lobsters).

Drain the lobster pieces and, when cool enough to handle, use nutcrackers to break open the shells. Remove the meat from the shell. If there is a visible dark vein on the underside of the tail, pull it off and discard. Chop the claw and tail meat into small chunks, and set aside to cool completely.

In a large bowl, whisk together the mayonnaise, lemon juice, Worcestershire sauce, garlic, chives, the remaining ½ teaspoon of salt, and the Tabasco sauce. Add the celery and the lobster meat and mix gently with the dressing. Chill for at least 30 minutes or up to 2 hours.

Melt the butter in your cleaned and dried Dutch oven (or in a large skillet) over medium heat. Add the buns and roll them around to coat with butter, cooking until lightly toasted on the outside. Spoon some lobster salad into each bun, garnish with the chives, and serve.

SERVES 4

2 1½- to 2-pound live lobsters
¼ cup plus ½ teaspoon kosher salt
1 cup mayonnaise
Juice of 1 lemon
1 teaspoon Worcestershire sauce
1 garlic clove, very finely chopped
1 tablespoon chopped fresh chives
Splash of Tabasco sauce
2 celery stalks, finely chopped
2 tablespoons unsalted butter
4 brioche rolls or hot dog buns, halved lengthwise but not all the way through
Chopped chives

BEER-BATTERED Cod *and* TARTAR SAUCE

Canola or grapeseed oil, for
    frying (1½ to 2 quarts)
1 12-ounce can or bottle of
    beer
2½ cups all-purpose flour
2 pounds cod, sliced crosswise
    into 4-inch-wide pieces
1 tablespoon kosher salt
Old-School Tartar Sauce (see
    page 70), for serving
2 lemons, cut into wedges,
    for serving

VINNY: We grew up eating lots of fish and chips in Florida. You can use almost any kind of semi-thick and mild white fish, such as haddock, grouper, fluke, or even tilapia. Out here in L.A., we like to use Pacific lingcod.

Jon: The beer batter is drippy, so when you fry the fish, you've got to "swim" it in. Just hold the fish with tongs, and shimmy it into the hot oil. Let the batter fry up and puff a bit before releasing the fillet all the way into the oil.

VINNY: We use whatever beer we have around: Red Stripe, Fat Tire, or even Pabst Blue Ribbon.

FILL your Dutch oven with 4 inches of oil and heat over high heat until it reaches 375°F. Line a plate with paper towels and set aside.

While the oil heats, whisk the beer and 2 cups of the flour together in a large bowl. The batter should be thick, like pancake batter. Place the remaining flour on a plate. Dredge the fish through the flour, tap off the excess, and then submerge in the batter. Allow the excess to drip off, and using a pair of tongs, slowly swim it into the hot oil. Once the batter starts to solidify and puff up a bit, release the fish into the hot oil. Fry the fish in two batches (so your oil doesn't cool down too much), turning the fish often to fry evenly on all sides until it is uniformly golden brown, 8 to 10 minutes. Transfer the fish to the paper towels to drain and season with some salt while still hot. (You can place the fish on a rimmed sheet pan and keep it warm in a 200°F oven while you fry the second batch.)

Place the fish on a platter or on individual plates and serve with tartar sauce and lemon wedges.

SERVES 4 TO 6

Duck Quarters *with* DRIED FRUIT *and* SHERRY

VINNY: I love duck confit, but making it at home is a whole lot of work and requires time and patience. This duck dish is the next best thing. The acidity of the fruit cuts through the duck's bold richness. It's awesome with a frisée salad or with frisée quickly sautéed in olive oil.

Jon: When you buy dried fruit, always give it a good look to make sure it doesn't have a powdery white bloom on its surface, a dead giveaway that the fruit has been sitting around for a long time. Old dried fruit has a nasty cardboardy texture and isn't as sweet.

PREHEAT your oven to 275°F.

Heat the oil in your Dutch oven over medium-high heat for 1 minute. Sprinkle the duck legs with 1 teaspoon of the salt and place them skin side down in the pot. Sear the duck legs until golden brown on both sides, about 12 minutes total. Transfer to a plate and set aside.

Pour off all but ½ tablespoon of fat from the pot (save the duck fat for roasting potatoes or caramelizing onions!) and add the shallots, garlic, and thyme to the pot. Cook until the garlic is fragrant, 1 to 2 minutes. Pour in the sherry wine and sherry vinegar, scraping any browned bits up from the bottom of the pot, and simmer until the shallots become translucent, about 5 minutes. Add the tomato paste, ½ cup water, and the remaining teaspoon of salt and cook for 1 minute. Add the dried fruit and the duck legs, along with any accumulated juices, to the pot.

Cover the pan and transfer to the oven. Bake until the meat easily falls from the bone, about 3 hours. Transfer the duck legs to a serving platter. Stir the butter into the sauce, then stir in the marjoram and parsley. Pour over the duck and serve.

SERVES 4

1 tablespoon canola or grapeseed oil

4 duck leg quarters (thighs and legs attached)

2 teaspoons kosher salt

5 shallots, halved and thinly sliced

3 garlic cloves, thinly sliced

3 fresh thyme sprigs

2 cups dry sherry

2 tablespoons sherry vinegar

1½ tablespoons tomato paste

½ cup dried black figs (about 10)

½ cup dried cherries

½ cup dried apricots

2 tablespoons unsalted butter

2 tablespoons finely chopped fresh marjoram

1 tablespoon finely chopped fresh flat-leaf parsley

AMATRICIANA-STYLE Chicken Legs *and* THIGHS

2 tablespoons olive oil

4 bone-in chicken legs

4 bone-in chicken thighs

1 tablespoon kosher salt

1 28-ounce can whole
tomatoes with liquid

1 cup finely chopped
pancetta (about 5 ounces)

1 yellow onion, finely
chopped

2 medium carrots, peeled and
finely chopped

4 garlic cloves, thinly sliced

¼ teaspoon red pepper flakes

2 cups dry white wine (such
as pinot grigio or
sauvignon blanc)

2 tablespoons unsalted butter

2 tablespoons finely grated
Pecorino cheese

1 tablespoon finely chopped
fresh flat-leaf parsley

This is our take on a classic Italian amatriciana, a sauce usually made with guanciale (unsmoked bacon made from pigs' cheeks) or pancetta, an Italian bacon. Unlike American bacon, however, pancetta doesn't get smoked, so it lends a subtler porky flavor to dishes. It's cool to have in the fridge because it has a pretty long shelf life of about three weeks. Freezing it makes it really easy to slice or chop. Use it to flavor food as you would use bacon. It's especially great in pasta, hearty soups, and rustic dishes like this one.

PREHEAT your oven to 350°F.

Heat the olive oil in a Dutch oven over medium-high heat for 1 minute. Season the chicken pieces with half of the salt and add to the pot, skin side down. Sear the chicken on all sides until golden brown, 10 to 12 minutes total. Transfer to a plate and discard the fat in the pan.

Pour the tomatoes into a large bowl and, using your hands, shred them into small bits. Set aside.

Reduce the heat to medium, add the pancetta to the pot, and scrape up all the browned bits off of the bottom of the pan. Cook until golden brown and crisp, about 5 minutes. Add the onions and cook until they begin to soften, 2 to 4 minutes. Add the carrots and cook until the vegetables are slightly browned, another 5 minutes. Stir in the garlic and red pepper flakes and cook until the garlic is fragrant, another 1 or 2 minutes. Stir in the wine and scrape up any browned bits from the bottom of the pot, then add the tomatoes and the remaining ½ tablespoon of salt and bring to a simmer.

Return the chicken to the pot along with any accumulated juices, cover, and bake until the chicken is tender and falls easily off the bone, about 1½ hours. Transfer the chicken to a serving platter. Stir the butter into the sauce and pour the sauce over the chicken. Sprinkle with the cheese and parsley and serve.

SERVES 4

our garlic bread

Adjust an oven rack to the upper-middle position and preheat the oven to 500°F. Slice 1 loaf of crusty Italian bread in half horizontally (like you would to make a sub sandwich). Mix together ¾ cup of mayonnaise, ½ cup of finely grated Parmigiano-Reggiano cheese, ¼ cup finely chopped garlic, 1 tablespoon dried oregano, 1½ teaspoons dried basil, and ¼ teaspoon freshly ground black pepper. Spread the paste on the cut sides of the bread, place the bread on a baking sheet, and bake until the edges are crisp, 7 to 9 minutes. Turn the broiler on to high and broil the loaves until they are golden, 1 to 2 minutes. Slice each half into pieces and serve.

tip

We like to use canned whole tomatoes and hand-shred them ourselves rather than using already chopped or diced tomatoes. The irregular texture you get from hand-shredding provides for a much nicer texture than the mechanically chopped alternative, and the shredding only adds two or three minutes to your prep time. Plus it's fun to get your hands dirty once in a while!

BUTTERMILK-SAGE Fried CHICKEN

6 boneless skin-on chicken breasts or thighs

2 cups buttermilk

1 cup all-purpose flour (plus more if needed)

10 fresh sage leaves, roughly chopped

3 cups canola oil

1 tablespoon kosher salt

Jon: I'm a nut for buttermilk-brined fried chicken. If you've never had fried chicken that has first been soaked in buttermilk, do yourself a favor and try it. The acid in the buttermilk breaks down the tissues in the chicken and makes the meat super tender. It's so cool: all you have to do is pull the chicken from the buttermilk, toss it in a little flour, and fry it. The buttermilk does all the work for you.

VINNY: This is one of our most requested dishes. People love it because there's no bone to deal with. If you decide to make it using bone-in chicken, be sure to let it brine for three days. It will also need to cook a little longer in the pot.

PLACE the chicken in a large resealable plastic bag with the buttermilk and refrigerate for at least 2 and up to 3 days.

In a large, shallow dish, mix the flour and sage together. One piece at a time, remove the chicken from the buttermilk, allowing any excess liquid to drip off, and then dredge through the flour, tapping off any excess. Place the coated chicken piece on a plate and repeat with the remaining pieces.

Heat the canola oil in a Dutch oven over high heat until it reaches 375°F on a digital thermometer. Add the chicken pieces to the pot (all of the chicken should fit in a single layer in the pot; if it doesn't, fry the chicken in two batches) and cook until the chicken is golden brown all over and cooked through, 8 to 10 minutes. Transfer to a paper-towel-lined plate to drain. Season with the salt while still hot and serve warm, at room temperature, or cold.

SERVES 3 OR 4

BUCATINI Carbonara, PANCETTA, *and* PEAS

2 tablespoons plus 1 teaspoon
    kosher salt

1 pound bucatini pasta

1 10-ounce bag frozen peas

1 teaspoon olive oil

8 ounces pancetta, sliced
    ¼ inch thick and finely
    diced

2 Spanish onions, very finely
    chopped

2 whole garlic cloves

1 cup dry white wine (such as
    pinot grigio or sauvignon
    blanc)

2½ cups heavy cream

2 large egg yolks

1 cup finely grated Pecorino
    cheese

1½ teaspoons finely ground
    black pepper

JON: Every cook ought to know how to make four or five great pasta dishes. Pasta carbonara should be one of them. It's a real Italian classic.

VINNY: Bucatini is similar to spaghetti except it has a hollow center that gives it great chew and allows the creamy sauce to get inside. It's a really beautiful pasta.

FILL a Dutch oven with water and bring to a boil. Add the 2 tablespoons of salt and the pasta and cook until the pasta is nearly al dente but still slightly undercooked. Add the peas to the pot and cook until the pasta is al dente and the peas are tender, another 1 or 2 minutes. Drain the pasta mixture and keep warm.

Wash out the pot and add the oil. Heat over medium-high heat. Once the oil is hot, add half of the pancetta and cook, stirring often, until browned and crisp on all sides, about 10 minutes. Transfer to a paper-towel-lined plate and set aside. Pour off the fat and discard.

Add the remaining pancetta and the onions and cook, stirring often, over medium-high heat until the onions are soft, 2 to 4 minutes. Stir in the garlic and, once it is fragrant, add the white wine. Simmer for 1 minute, then add the cream. Simmer the cream until it has reduced slightly, about 10 minutes, and stir in the remaining 1 teaspoon of salt. Reduce the heat to the lowest setting.

Place the egg yolks in a small bowl or coffee cup and whisk in a few tablespoons of the hot cream mixture. When well blended, whisk in a few more tablespoons of the cream. This will warm the egg yolks so they don't curdle when you add them to the sauce. Whisk the egg yolk mixture into the cream sauce and remove and discard the garlic.

Add the pasta and the reserved crispy pancetta to the sauce. Stir in three quarters of the cheese and the black pepper and place in a serving bowl or in individual bowls. Sprinkle each serving with a little of the remaining cheese and serve.

SERVES 4 TO 6

no joke: raw yolks

Raw egg yolks are an important part of this dish. Besides adding a nice warm color to the sauce, they add richness and thickness, too. We don't get it: people eat sunny-side-up eggs or raw cookie batter, but they freak out about raw egg yolks in pasta sauce or eggnog. If they really turn you off of the recipe, then omit the raw yolks and add 2 tablespoons of cream to the total cream amount. You may have to cook the cream a little longer to get a nice, thick consistency. If, however, you are pregnant or immunosuppressed or are making carbonara for young children or the elderly, then you should omit the raw eggs.

SLOW-COOKED Lamb Shanks *in* PINOT NOIR

2 tablespoons olive oil

4 lamb shanks, ¾ to 1 pound each

3 teaspoons kosher salt

1 28-ounce can whole tomatoes with liquid

1 yellow onion, finely chopped

1 fennel bulb, fronds and stalks removed, halved, cored, and thinly sliced

2 carrots, peeled and chopped into 1½-inch lengths (optional)

4 garlic cloves, thinly sliced

1 lemon, halved

1½ cups pinot noir

1½ teaspoons finely grated peeled fresh ginger

2 cinnamon sticks

1 teaspoon whole coriander seeds

1 teaspoon fennel seeds

3 tablespoons unsalted butter

12 fresh mint leaves

Jon: This is the kind of hearty winter dish that makes your whole house smell amazing. It's great to make when you're having friends over for dinner. For a side dish I like to sauté the same vegetables we use to cook the lamb—fennel, carrots, onions—and mix them into couscous.

VINNY: Jonny likes this with carrots, but I think he's nuts; it's way better without. It's one of the few dishes that we part ways on! We both agree that it's awesome with couscous or even Israeli (pearl) couscous, and I like it with cooked wheat berries, too.

PREHEAT your oven to 300°F.

Heat the olive oil in a Dutch oven over medium-high heat. Sprinkle the lamb with 2 teaspoons of the salt and brown in the hot oil on all sides. Remove the lamb to a plate and pour off any excess fat from the pan.

Pour the tomatoes into a large bowl and, using your hands, shred them into small pieces. Set aside.

Add the onions, fennel, carrots (if using), garlic, and the remaining 1 teaspoon of salt to the pot. Cook, stirring and scraping any browned bits off the bottom of the pot, until the garlic is lightly toasted, 3 to 4 minutes. Squeeze in the lemon juice from each half and toss the lemon rinds into the pot. Stir in the wine, tomatoes, and ginger, scraping any browned bits up from the bottom of the pot, and bring to a simmer; cook for about 3 minutes.

Stir in the cinnamon, coriander, fennel seeds, and ¾ cup water, then add the lamb to the pot. Cover and bake in the oven until the lamb is fork-tender and falls easily off the bone, about 3 hours.

Arrange the lamb shanks on a platter. Stir the butter into the pan juices and, once melted, add the mint. Pour the sauce over the lamb, discard the cinnamon sticks, and serve.

SERVES 4 TO 6

squeezing lemons

One of the easiest ways to extract lemon juice without having to deal with seeds is to squeeze a lemon half over your cupped hand. Let the lemon juice drip between your fingers and keep the seeds in your hand.

tip

This is the kind of food that tastes even better the day after it is made. Make it one to two days in advance for the best flavor, or eat it the day you make it and hide the leftovers for something to look forward to in a day or two.

WHITE Wine–Braised OSSO BUCO

2 tablespoons olive oil

4 pounds cross-cut veal shanks or "osso buco" (preferably center-cut)

2 teaspoons kosher salt

1 28-ounce can whole tomatoes with liquid

8 ounces button mushrooms, stems removed and caps thinly sliced

1 yellow onion, finely chopped

5 whole, peeled garlic cloves

3 celery stalks, finely chopped

1 carrot, peeled and grated

1½ cups dry white wine (such as pinot grigio or sauvignon blanc)

2 tablespoons unsalted butter

1½ tablespoons finely chopped fresh basil

1 tablespoon finely chopped fresh flat-leaf parsley

1 teaspoon finely chopped fresh thyme

Jon: The best parts of osso buco are the marrow in the bone and the sauce. I totally get on that bone! And the sauce is amazing with grilled bread or Israeli (pearl) couscous.

VINNY: I grew up sucking marrow out of bones. There's something so carnal and cool about eating bones.

PREHEAT your oven to 300°F.

Heat the oil in a Dutch oven over medium-high heat. Season the veal with 1½ teaspoons of the salt and sear until golden brown on all sides, about 12 minutes. Transfer the veal to a plate and pour off the fat in the pan.

Pour the tomatoes into a large bowl and, using your hands, shred them into small pieces. Set aside.

Add the mushrooms, onions, garlic, and remaining ½ teaspoon of salt to the pot and cook, stirring often, until the garlic is lightly toasted, 2 to 3 minutes. Remove and discard the garlic cloves and add the celery, carrots, and wine, stirring and scraping any browned bits up from the bottom of the pot. Bring to a simmer, then add the tomatoes and 1 cup water. Bring to a simmer again and return the veal to the pot along with any accumulated juices.

two-for-one
We like to make double portions of slow-cooked food, even if it means putting two pots in the oven at the same time. After cooling it to room temperature, we portion out and freeze whatever is extra. You can serve it as is, or shred the meat and use it for sandwiches, tacos or taquitos, or crostini (see page 164).

Reduce the heat to medium-low, cover the pot, and transfer to the oven. Bake until the veal is fork-tender, about 3½ to 4 hours. Arrange the veal in a serving dish. Stir the butter into the sauce until it is melted, then stir in the basil, parsley, and thyme and serve.

SERVES 4 TO 6

saffron risotto

Saffron Risotto, also called Risotto Milanese, is the classic accompaniment to osso buco. To make it, follow the recipe for Asparagus Risotto on page 138. Leave out the asparagus and instead stir in ¼ teaspoon of crushed saffron (place a generous pinch of saffron threads in a small dish and grind them into a powder using the back of a metal teaspoon).

tip

Gremolata is the classic accompaniment to osso buco. Its fresh, bright flavors really cut through the richness of the veal. Mix together ¼ cup finely chopped fresh flat-leaf parsley, 2 teaspoons very finely chopped garlic, 1 teaspoon finely grated lemon zest, and 1 teaspoon finely grated orange zest. Sprinkled over the osso buco and serve.

VINNY'S SPAGHETTI BOLOGNESE

2 tablespoons olive oil

2 medium carrots, peeled and very finely chopped

1 small yellow onion, very finely chopped

1 celery stalk, very finely chopped

3 garlic cloves, very finely chopped

5 ounces pancetta, finely chopped

12 ounces ground chuck

12 ounces ground veal

12 ounces ground pork

1½ cups dry white wine (such as pinot grigio or sauvignon blanc)

5 tablespoons tomato paste

3 cups whole milk

1½ teaspoons finely chopped fresh thyme

2 tablespoons plus 2 teaspoons kosher salt, plus more if needed

1 pound spaghetti

2 tablespoons heavy cream

1 tablespoon unsalted butter

Freshly grated Parmigiano-Reggiano cheese, for serving

Jon: If you think that Bolognese is a tomato sauce with some ground beef in it, then you're in for a bomb-ass surprise! This sauce is tricked out with ingredients that combine to make it seriously delicious. Freeze whatever is left over and pull it out when you crave something really fine. When Vin steps up to the stove to make his Bolognese, I know to clear the area; he gets really intense when he's making it.

VINNY: I eat pasta Bolognese at least once a week; it's definitely my number one favorite pasta dish.

HEAT the oil in a large Dutch oven over medium-high heat. Add the chopped carrots, onions, celery, and garlic and cook, stirring often, until the vegetables begin to soften, about 4 minutes. Add the pancetta and cook, stirring often, until it is just starting to brown, 3 to 5 minutes.

Stir in the ground meats and cook, stirring often, until they begin to brown, about 8 minutes. Pour in the white wine, bring to a simmer, and cook for 2 minutes. Stir in the tomato paste and, once incorporated, add the milk, thyme, and 2 teaspoons of salt. Bring to a simmer, then reduce the heat to low (the sauce should occasionally bubble) and cook until thick, about 1½ hours, stirring often so the sauce doesn't brown on the bottom. Remove from the heat and keep covered until ready to serve.

Bring a large pot of water to a boil. Add 2 tablespoons of salt and the pasta and cook according to the box instructions until the pasta is al dente; drain. Stir the cream and butter into the sauce until completely incorporated. Taste for seasoning and add salt if necessary. Place the pasta in a serving bowl and toss with the sauce. Serve with lots of grated Parm.

SERVES 8

salting like the ocean

Our benchmark for salting large amounts of water—whether for boiling pasta, green beans, or potatoes—is to salt the water so it tastes like the ocean. Not too salty like the Gulf of Mexico, just a nice salty—more Atlantic than Pacific, if you know what we mean.

Beer-Braised SHORT RIBS and SHIITAKES

VINNY: Tomatoes are a great tenderizer, whether in the form of fresh chopped tomatoes, tomato paste, or ketchup. The acids in tomatoes help to break down proteins in meat. We use ketchup in this recipe because we like the sweet-tangy element it brings to the sauce.

Jon: Don't be bummed out at the thought of pouring a can of beer into the pan. As much good as you could've gotten from that beer, the short ribs get more!

PREHEAT your oven to 300°F.

Heat the oil in a large Dutch oven over medium-high heat. Sprinkle the short ribs with 1 tablespoon of the salt and cook until browned on all sides, 10 to 12 minutes. Place the short ribs on a plate and pour off all but 1 tablespoon of fat from the pan.

Add the mushrooms, carrots, onions, and turnips and cook, stirring and scraping any browned bits up off the bottom of the pan, until the onions start to soften, about 4 minutes. Stir in the remaining ½ tablespoon of salt, and then add 2 cups water, the beer, soy sauce, brown sugar, ketchup, garlic, star anise, and red pepper flakes, stirring and scraping any browned bits up from the bottom of the pot. Bring to a simmer, then return the short ribs and any accumulated juices back to the pot. Cover and place in the oven. Bake until the short ribs fall off the bone in tender chunks, about 3 hours.

Transfer the short ribs and the sauce to a platter or a wide, shallow bowl and serve.

SERVES 6 TO 8

2 tablespoons canola or grapeseed oil

4 pounds bone-in beef short ribs

1½ tablespoons kosher salt

20 shiitake mushroom caps (about 3 cups)

1 large carrot, peeled and finely chopped

1 red onion, finely chopped

1 medium turnip, peeled and finely chopped

1 12-ounce can of beer (we like Sapporo here)

¼ cup soy sauce

½ cup light brown sugar

¼ cup ketchup

5 whole garlic cloves

5 whole star anise

½ teaspoon red pepper flakes

. . . VARIATION

JON'S SHORT RIB AND MASHED POTATO CROSTINI

When I was fifteen years old and a dishwasher in Florida, I used to eat short rib and mashed potato sandwiches all the time. This sandwich is what first turned me on to good food, and it is also a great use for leftover short ribs and mashed potatoes (see page 133). We make a more refined version for parties, but these are just as satisfying.

Cut a baguette on the diagonal into ¼-inch-thick slices. Brush with some olive oil and toast in a 350°F oven until lightly browned. Spread with some mashed potatoes and top with some shredded short ribs. Finish the dish with a dollop of crème fraîche and some chopped chives, if you like.

tip

Short ribs come from the chuck and are 2- to 4-inch-long chunks of meat and fat attached to a rib. You can get flanken short ribs, which are usually 3-inch-long pieces that are cut across the bone (so you'll see three or four small pieces of rib in each short rib) or English-style short ribs that are about 4 inches long and are cut along the length of the rib. Because they're tough and fatty and require slow, low cooking to properly coax out their amazing, deep, beefy flavor and melt-in-your-mouth texture, they're a deal to buy, usually costing less than $6 a pound (though boneless short ribs cost more). Flanken short ribs are easier to find, so that's the cut that we cook with the most.

"BIG RED" *with* Brisket *and* PINTO BEANS

Hearty with a lot of body, this is kind of an everything-but-the-kitchen-sink version of chili. It's flavorful and bold, with chunks of brisket, beans, ground beef, and bacon for a smoky edge. This is winter food at its best. Make a big batch and freeze the leftovers in individual portions for chili on the fly. We also love this chili on hot dogs and French fries!

HEAT a Dutch oven over medium-high heat for 1 minute. Add the bacon pieces and cook, stirring often, until browned and crisp, 8 to 10 minutes. Use a slotted spoon to transfer the bacon to a paper-towel-lined plate and set aside.

Pour off all but 1 tablespoon of the bacon fat. Cut the brisket in 1-inch cubes, add to the pot, and cook until browned on all sides, about 5 minutes total. Add the onions, garlic, and 1 teaspoon of the salt to the pot and cook, stirring often, until the onions are soft, about 3 minutes. Stir in the ground beef and cook, stirring often, until browned, about 5 minutes.

Pour the tomatoes into a large bowl and, using your hands, shred them into small pieces. Add the tomatoes, 1 cup of water, the remaining teaspoon of salt, and the remaining chili ingredients to the pot. Stir well, bring to a simmer, reduce the heat to low (barely simmering with an occasional bubble), and cook until the brisket is fall-apart tender and the chili is thick, about 3½ hours. Serve in big bowls and sprinkle with the grated Cheddar and chopped onions.

SERVES 10 TO 12

FOR THE CHILI

8 ounces bacon, cut in
¼-inch-wide pieces
1 pound beef brisket
2 yellow onions, finely
chopped
3 garlic cloves, smashed
2 teaspoons kosher salt
1½ pounds ground chuck
1 28-ounce can whole
tomatoes with liquid
3 14-ounce cans pinto beans,
drained and rinsed
1 12-ounce bottle of beer
1 cup ketchup
¼ cup light brown sugar
2 tablespoons tomato paste
1½ tablespoons
Worcestershire sauce
2 teaspoons white vinegar
1 teaspoon Tabasco sauce
2½ tablespoons chili powder
1 tablespoon ground cumin
1 tablespoon dried oregano
1 teaspoon cayenne pepper
1½ teaspoons garlic powder
1½ teaspoons onion powder

FOR SERVING

Grated Cheddar cheese
Chopped white onions

ROASTING
PAN

VINNY: Roasting is one of the simplest ways to cook. It's approachable, requires very little hands-on attention, and creates great-tasting food with a gorgeous color and deep flavor. This chapter offers some solid basics to work off of: roast chicken, a roast pork butt, and even roast fish. Once you nail the method, you can add your favorite herbs or flavorings to own the dish.

Jon: I've always liked the fact that roasting leaves you with a clean stovetop.

VINNY: Yeah, you're lazy that way!

Jon: No, really: all the work gets done in the oven, so your cooking surface is free to whip up a side dish.

VINNY: It's also cool because you can cook using really high heat. When we're pressed for time, nothing beats it, and it gives most meat a nice crisp crust.

Jon: In our kitchen, we use restaurant-grade hotel pans that are built to take a beating. We work them hard! To extend their lifespan, we soak them in warm, soapy water and scrub them down until they're sparkling. Treat your roasting pan right, and it should last you a long time.

VINNY: Oh, this is a cool trick too—if you don't have a great roasting pan, place it on top of a baking sheet before roasting. The baking sheet will help to distribute the heat evenly, preventing your meat or vegetables from burning.

Jon: A good roasting pan is pricey, but it's definitely worth the investment!

VINNY: Another thing that's important when roasting is to rest your meat when it comes out of the oven. Transfer it from the roasting pan to a cutting board (follow Jon's advice for cleaning the pan; we're sticklers for cleanliness) and loosely cover it with aluminum foil. Let it hang out for 10 to 20 minutes. This rest allows the juices to get reabsorbed into the meat. If you carve a roast too soon, the juices will run all over, leaving your meat parched.

Jon: This is important too: pull the meat out of the oven when it's a little underdone. The meat will continue to cook while it's resting. This is called carryover heat. If you wait until the meat is cooked exactly the way you want it, you run the risk of it becoming overcooked during its rest period. There's nothing worse than an overcooked piece of meat, no matter what cut it is.

VINNY: Roast leg of lamb, roast pork chops, a prime rib roast. These dishes are classics for a reason. Master them, and you'll always have something impressive to put on the table for a holiday celebration, dinner party, or supper with the family.

MENU

Salt-Roasted *Baby* POTATOES

DRESSED, ROASTED TOMATOES *with* **Burrata**

Miso EGGPLANT

Spicy **Roasted Cauliflower,** CAPERS, *and* PARM

ROASTED PEPPERS, **Goat Cheese,** *and* Pine Nuts

SEA BASS, **Clams, Bacon,** *and* **Leeks** *in* WHITE WINE

Sherried Salmon *and* CIPOLLINI ONIONS

FIVE-SPICE **Cornish Hens**

Lemon-Sage ROASTED CHICKEN

CIDER-SAGE **Pork Chops**

Chile-Rubbed PORK LOIN

Balsamic **BARBECUED Baby Backs**

Cuban-Style ROAST PORK

Rosemary-Garlic Marinated LEG *of* LAMB

HARISSA–RUBBED Rack *of* Lamb *with* MINT YOGURT

LONDON BROIL *with* Herb Butter

Garlic-Herb Crusted PRIME RIB *with* Madeira Sauce

BACON–WRAPPED Meatloaf

Roasted Bones *with* PARSLEY, TOAST, *and* AGED BALSAMIC

SALT-ROASTED
Baby POTATOES

2 3-pound boxes of
   kosher salt
2 pounds whole baby
   potatoes (red bliss, Yukon
   Golds, fingerlings, purple
   Peruvians)
2 teaspoons canola or
   grapeseed oil
¼ cup sour cream
2 tablespoons finely chopped
   fresh chives

VINNY: We salt-roast all kinds of tubers and root vegetables, including sweet potatoes, rutabaga, and turnips. The dry heat makes them seriously creamy and accentuates their natural sweetness and amazing flavor.

Jon: This is one of the best techniques I learned at Chadwick's restaurant, where Vin and I worked soon after we moved to L.A. When chef Govind Armstrong showed me how to make this, I filed it away in my book of tricks. Two boxes of salt may seem like a lot, but you're not seasoning the potatoes with it; you're using the salt to cushion the potatoes in the pan.

PREHEAT your oven to 375°F. Pour the salt into a roasting pan, mounding it in the center so the potatoes have a ½-inch-deep bed to roast on.

Toss the potatoes with the oil in a large bowl. Arrange them on the salt and cover the pan tightly with aluminum foil, crimping it around the edges. Roast the potatoes until a paring knife easily pierces the center of a potato and the potato is tender all the way through, 45 minutes to 1 hour and 15 minutes (the roasting time varies depending on the kind of potato you're roasting and how big it is).

Remove the potatoes from the oven and let cool for 15 minutes. Brush off the salt and transfer them to a cutting board. Halve the potatoes lengthwise and sprinkle them with salt. Divide them among 8 plates and serve with dollops of sour cream and a sprinkling of chives.

SERVES 8

SIZZLE PLATES

Jon: A sizzle plate looks like a fajita pan—it's oval, metal, and very shallow.

VINNY: Sizzle plates are like an extension of your arm in pro kitchens. We use them for everything. They're great for oven-roasting one or two portions of food. The plate's small surface area lets it get hot really fast.

Jon: I like stainless-steel sizzles because they're easy to maneuver, and they can go from oven to table. Unlike cast-iron and nonstick pans, you can scrub them without worrying about taking off their coating. Plus, they're really cheap; you can find them online or at restaurant supply stores for less than fifteen dollars apiece.

VINNY: They remind me of those old-school steak houses with massive double-decker broilers they load up with stacks and stacks of steaks on sizzle plates. They're totally badass!

Jon: Be careful when you take a sizzle plate out of the oven because they get really hot. Make sure there is a dry kitchen towel or oven mitt standing by.

VINNY: Also, check the food often, because no two oven-broilers cook alike. Turn around for a minute or two too long and your food is carbonized. Once you're comfortable with it, though, it really is a great cooking tool.

Jon: Almost all of the recipes from this chapter can be adapted to a sizzle plate if you cut the serving portions down to two. For example, divide the ingredients for the Sherried Salmon and Cipollini Onions (page 186) by three to get the quantity for two servings; for the Five-Spice Cornish Hens (page 187), you'd divide the ingredients in half.

Some other recipes from the book that work great on a sizzle plate are:
- Grouper with Lemon-Caper Butter, page 104
- Salt-Roasted Baby Potatoes, page 172
- Cider-Sage Pork Chops, page 190
- Harissa-Rubbed Rack of Lamb, page 200

Dressed, Roasted TOMATOES
with BURRATA

1 tablespoon olive oil for
    greasing the pan
10 plum tomatoes, halved
¼ cup plus 2 tablespoons
    good-quality extra-virgin
    olive oil
1½ teaspoons kosher salt
10 fresh thyme sprigs
2 4-ounce balls burrata
    cheese, each ball
    quartered
8 fresh basil leaves

tip

This is a really simple yet beautiful dish in which the quality of each ingredient stands out. Pull out your good olive oil for this one, and if you don't have any, this is a great excuse to buy some. Make it a fruity, green olive oil; the burrata and the tomatoes can totally take it on.

Jon: Burrata is like fresh mozzarella with a twist. On the outside, it's *mozzarella di bufala* (mozzarella made with water buffalo milk). Slice into it and you release this insane creamy center made from a combination of mozzarella and heavy cream. It's so delicious and makes this dish really special, but if you can't find it, any nice fresh mozzarella will work.

VINNY: When I learned how easy it is to make roasted tomatoes and how awesome they taste, I freaked out and started using them everywhere: in salads, on burgers, and added to tomato sauce. I just buzz them right in using an immersion blender to intensify the flavor.

PREHEAT your oven to 175°F. Grease a roasting pan with olive oil or pan spray.

Toss the tomatoes in a large bowl with the ¼ cup of olive oil and 1 teaspoon of the salt. Place the tomatoes in the roasting pan cut side down and scatter the thyme sprigs throughout. Roast until still moist but shrunken in size by at least half, 3 to 4 hours, and then set aside to cool. (Switch on your oven light every hour or so to make sure they're not browning.) Once they are cool, slip the skins off of the tomatoes.

Place 2 cheese quarters on each of 4 plates. Top each piece of cheese with a tomato, drizzle with a little of the remaining olive oil, and sprinkle with the remaining ½ teaspoon of salt. Top with the basil and serve.

SERVES 4

MISO EGGPLANT

Jon: This eggplant could convert me to being a vegetarian, it's that good.

VINNY: It is good—but it couldn't convert me to being a vegetarian!

PREHEAT your oven to 500°F. Line a roasting pan with aluminum foil and set aside.

Toss the eggplant with the oil and salt in a large bowl, then place them cut side down in the roasting pan. Roast until the eggplant skin becomes slightly hard, 5 to 7 minutes. Reduce the oven temperature to 350°F and roast until they are soft to the touch but still hold their shape, 2 to 4 minutes longer.

While the eggplant roasts, make the miso glaze. Place the miso, brown sugar, 2 tablespoons water, the vinegar, and soy sauce in a medium bowl and whisk to combine.

Remove the pan from the oven and set aside until the eggplant is cool enough to flip with your fingers, 1 to 2 minutes (you can use tongs if you like, but be very gentle so you don't break the soft skin). Brush some glaze over the cut side of each eggplant.

Turn the oven to broil and place the oven rack as close to the broiler heating element as you can. Broil the eggplant until the glaze is hot and bubbling, 30 seconds to 1 minute. (If you don't have a built-in broiling element in your oven, crank the oven heat to 500°F and roast the eggplant until the glaze is hot and bubbling.) Serve immediately.

SERVES 4 TO 6

1½ pounds Japanese eggplant (about 4), tops removed, halved lengthwise
1 tablespoon canola or grapeseed oil
1 teaspoon kosher salt
¼ cup yellow miso
3 tablespoons light brown sugar
1½ teaspoons rice vinegar
1½ teaspoons soy sauce

tip
Long and thin Japanese eggplant have a thicker skin than bulbous American globe eggplant. They're sweeter, too, so you don't need to salt them to draw out their bitterness before cooking. Italian eggplant is a good substitute.

SPICY ROASTED Cauliflower, CAPERS, *and* PARM

½ cup olive oil, plus
 1 tablespoon for
 greasing the pan
2 heads of cauliflower,
 trimmed into florets
 (about 12 cups florets)
2 teaspoons kosher salt
½ cup drained capers
1½ teaspoons red pepper
 flakes
½ cup finely grated
 Parmigiano-Reggiano
 cheese

Jon: My favorite part of this dish is the seriously roasted little bits left over in the pan after all of the bigger florets have been scooped up for serving. To make sure I get enough of them, I transfer every last nugget of cauliflower from the cutting board to my sheet pan before roasting.

VINNY: As a side dish or tossed into pasta, this is one of my favorite vegetable dishes. Take the sherry vinegar–soaked raisins from the carrot salad on page 38 and add them to the cauliflower with some fresh mint for a cool take on caponata.

PREHEAT your oven to 450°F. Grease a roasting pan with the 1 tablespoon of olive oil and set aside.

Place the cauliflower florets in a large bowl and toss with the ½ cup of olive oil and the salt. Transfer to the roasting pan and roast until deep golden brown, 25 to 35 minutes, stirring the cauliflower midway through cooking.

Remove the cauliflower from the oven and sprinkle with the capers and red pepper flakes, tossing together to combine. Transfer to a dish, sprinkle with the cheese, and serve.

SERVES 6

Roasted Peppers, GOAT CHEESE, and PINE NUTS

½ cup pine nuts

6 tablespoons olive oil, plus more for the pan

2 teaspoons kosher salt

6 large or 8 medium red or yellow bell peppers

2 tablespoons balsamic vinegar (preferably the white variety if you can find it)

2 shallots, very finely chopped

12 fresh basil leaves, finely chopped

2 ounces fresh goat cheese, crumbled

---

stand up straight
If your peppers have somewhat flat bottoms, then roast them upright. They'll roast more evenly and you won't have to turn them while cooking.

VINNY: We do roasted peppers the old-school way: in the oven. A lot of people roast them on the stovetop or even under the broiler, but they're sweeter this way.

Jon: Watch those pine nuts when you toast them and be sure to buy double what you need, just in case they burn.

PREHEAT your oven to 450°F. Place the pine nuts in a roasting pan and toast in the oven until browned and fragrant, 5 to 8 minutes, shaking the roasting pan midway through cooking. Transfer the nuts to a bowl and set aside.

Combine 2 tablespoons oil and 1½ teaspoons salt in a large bowl. Pierce each pepper with the tip of a knife and toss to coat with the oil. Drizzle some oil into the pan; add the peppers and any accumulated oil to the pan. Roast until charred and blistered on all sides, turning the peppers every 6 minutes, for 20 to 25 minutes total.

Transfer the peppers to a bowl, cover with plastic wrap, and set aside until they are cool. Peel the charred skins off of the peppers. Slice each pepper open and remove the seeds and fibers, and slice the peppers into quarters.

Place ¼ cup olive oil, the balsamic, shallots, basil, and ½ teaspoon salt in a gallon-size resealable plastic bag; shake to combine. Add the peppers and turn in the marinade to coat. Refrigerate for at least 30 minutes or up to 3 days.

To serve, place a few pepper quarters on each plate. Sprinkle with pine nuts and goat cheese. Drizzle with a little of the marinade.

SERVES 6 TO 8

RIMMED BAKING SHEET PANS

Jon: One thing every cook should invest in is a sturdy 18 by 13-inch sheet pan with a rimmed edge on all four sides.

VINNY: Rimmed sheet pans are the workhorses of every pro kitchen. You can use them for everything, from roasting chickens to baking cookies.

Jon: We like professional half-sheets for home cooks, rather than full sheet pans, which measure 26 by 18 inches. Half-sheets fit in most ovens (I know so many people who have loaded up a full-size sheet pan and then couldn't get it in their oven!) and their sides contain whatever is on the pan.

VINNY: That's the main difference between cookie sheets and half-sheets, also known as baking sheets. Cookie sheets don't have sides, so there's no way to keep a stray asparagus spear or baby potato from rolling right off. The rimmed sides of half-sheets hold everything in, including roasting juices given off by, say, a meatloaf or chicken.

Jon: The edge also gives you a lip to hook aluminum foil onto if you need to cover the pan for some reason.

VINNY: They stack easily, they're cheap, they're sturdy. Get a few. You'll definitely use them.

Jon: To keep the pan in good shape, line it with a piece of kitchen parchment or one of those silicone mats before cooking anything off. It will help prevent food from sticking to the pan, and it makes cleanup a heck of a lot easier. Greasing the sheet pan with oil or pan spray gets the job done, too, although greasing the pan adds to your cleanup post cooking.

VINNY: And a sheet pan is a fraction of the price of a decent roasting pan. If you're just beginning to build your cookware collection, start with the sheet pan and graduate to the roasting pan. They work especially well for smaller, shorter items such as tomatoes or ribs, because they expose the food to more hot air than a deep roasting pan does.

Jon: Another plus is that you can get food really close to the broiler element in your oven for a final blast of heat.

recipes that can also work on a sheet pan include:

- Salt-Roasted Baby Potatoes, page 172
- Dressed, Roasted Tomatoes with Burrata, page 174
- Miso Eggplant, page 177
- Spicy Roasted Cauliflower, Capers, and Parm, page 178
- Roasted Peppers, Goat Cheese, and Pine Nuts, page 180
- Balsamic Barbecued Baby Backs, page 194
- Bacon-Wrapped Meatloaf, page 203
- Roasted Bones with Parsley, Toast, and Aged Balsamic, page 205

SEA BASS, Clams, BACON, and Leeks in WHITE WINE

8 bacon strips, thinly sliced crosswise

2 garlic cloves, thinly sliced

6 leeks, white part only, halved lengthwise and thinly sliced

2 teaspoons kosher salt

6 6- to 8-ounce sea bass fillets

1½ teaspoons finely chopped fresh thyme

20 littleneck or cherrystone clams

¼ teaspoon red pepper flakes

1½ cups dry white wine (such as pinot grigio or sauvignon blanc)

2 tablespoons unsalted butter

2 lemons cut into wedges, for serving

Jon: A lot of people don't think about roasting clams, but they're so amazing done this way. The clams open right in the pot, adding a fantastic depth of flavor to the sauce. It's very cool.

VINNY: A side dish of chickpeas or corn hash (see page 82) really complements the flavors and textures of bacon with shellfish, fish, and leeks. When you halve the leeks, be sure to fan the tops and bottoms under cold running water so any sediment or dirt tucked in there gets rinsed out.

PREHEAT your oven to 350°F.

Place the sliced bacon in a roasting pan and bake it until it is browned and crisp, stirring often, 10 to 12 minutes. Stir in the garlic and roast until it becomes fragrant and is just starting to brown, 1 to 2 minutes. Stir in the leeks, sprinkle with ½ teaspoon of the salt, and continue to roast, stirring occasionally, until they start to soften, 4 to 5 minutes.

Season the fish fillets with half of the thyme and the remaining 1½ teaspoons of salt and set aside. Stir the remaining thyme into the leeks, then add the clams and sprinkle them with the red pepper flakes. Set the fish on top of the clams, pour the wine around the edges of the roasting pan, and return to the oven until the fish is firm and flakes easily and the clams are open, 8 to 10 minutes.

Divide the clams and fish among 6 bowls (discard any clams that don't open). Stir the butter into the leeks and spoon the sauce over the fish. Serve with the lemon wedges.

SERVES 6

SHERRIED Salmon and Cipollini ONIONS

FOR THE GLAZE

6 tablespoons sherry vinegar
1 tablespoon plus 1½ teaspoons grainy mustard
2 tablespoons honey

FOR THE SALMON

1½ pounds cipollini onions, peeled, or small shallots, peeled and halved
¼ cup canola or grapeseed oil
1 tablespoon plus 1½ teaspoons kosher salt
6 6- to 8-ounce salmon fillets (skin removed)

Jon: Sometimes when you're cooking salmon in the oven, the house gets a little fishy, you know? You won't get that with this recipe. Instead, the sherry makes makes the house smell amazing. This is a great recipe for anyone new to cooking fish because you just put the fillets on the onions and let them roast, no turning necessary.

VINNY: Salmon is cool because it's like a clean slate that you can add a ton of different flavors to, kind of like chicken. Watch out for the farmed salmon with added color. We'll use frozen wild salmon over artificially colored fresh salmon any day.

PREHEAT your oven to 500°F.

Whisk the vinegar, mustard, and honey together in a small bowl and set aside.

Place the onions or shallots in a bowl and toss with the oil and the 1½ teaspoons of salt. Transfer them to a roasting pan and roast until the onions are caramelized and browned all over and starting to get soft, 10 to 15 minutes, stirring midway through cooking.

Season all sides of the salmon with the remaining tablespoon of salt and arrange the fish on top of the onions. Brush the fish with the glaze and roast it until the fillets are golden brown on top and spring back to semifirm pressure, 8 to 10 minutes (check the fish often, as oven heat varies). Remove from the oven and serve with the onions on the side.

SERVES 6

FIVE-SPICE CORNISH Hens

Jon: Stay away from seasoned rice vinegar and seasoned mirin. They give the vinaigrette a nasty taste.

VINNY: If you're feeling like something a little different, swap the hen for squab. It has a gamier flavor.

PLACE a roasting pan on your oven's middle rack and preheat your oven to 450°F.

To make the hens, whisk the oil, five-spice powder, and salt together in a small bowl. Rub the mixture all over the Cornish hens and inside of the cavities. Divide the red onions, carrots, and cinnamon sticks equally among the hens' cavities, add the thyme sprigs, and plug each cavity with an orange half. Tie the legs together with a piece of butcher's twine and place the hens on a rack in the roasting pan.

Reduce the oven temperature to 425°F and roast the hens until the juices where the leg meets the body run clear when pierced with the tip of a knife and the hens are golden brown, 35 to 45 minutes.

Transfer the hens to a cutting board, tent them loosely with foil, and let them rest while you make the vinaigrette. Place the scallions and shallots in the roasting pan and let them sizzle for 15 seconds (if they don't sizzle, place the pan in the oven for 1 minute). Add the rice vinegar, mirin, honey, oil, and salt to the pan, stir to combine, and set aside.

Remove the orange halves, herbs, and vegetables from the hens' cavities. Arrange the hens on a serving platter or individual plates and squeeze the oranges over them. Drizzle with the vinaigrette and serve immediately.

SERVES 4

FOR THE HENS

¼ cup canola or grapeseed oil

3 tablespoons five-spice powder

2 teaspoons kosher salt

4 1- to 1½-pound Cornish game hens

1 large red onion, peeled and roughly chopped

1 large carrot, peeled, quartered, and cut in 1-inch lengths

2 cinnamon sticks, broken into 2 pieces

16 fresh thyme sprigs

2 oranges, halved

FOR THE VINAIGRETTE

4 scallions, white and light green parts only, thinly sliced on the diagonal

½ small shallot, finely diced

½ cup unseasoned rice vinegar

¼ cup unseasoned mirin

2 tablespoons honey

½ cup canola or grapeseed oil

2 teaspoons kosher salt

LEMON-SAGE ROASTED CHICKEN

VINNY: Everyone should have a recipe for a great roasted chicken. Tucking butter under the skin of the breast helps add richness and moistness to the white meat.

Jon: Roast chicken is great for dinner parties or for chill nights at home. We start it out at 450°F to give the skin an initial blast of heat so it gets nice and crisp.

PREHEAT your oven to 450°F.

Place the chicken on your cutting board. Slip your fingers under the skin of the breast and gently work them down the breast to create a pocket. Insert 1½ tablespoons of the butter and 3 sage leaves into each breast pocket. Rub the chicken with 1 tablespoon of the olive oil and then salt the cavity and the entire surface of the chicken.

Toss the sliced onions with the remaining 2 tablespoons of oil in a roasting pan and then evenly spread them over the bottom of the pan. Stuff the chicken with the thyme sprigs, the sage sprig, the quartered onion, and whole garlic cloves, and plug with the lemon halves. Tuck the wings under the breasts and set the chicken on top of the sliced onions.

Reduce the oven temperature to 425°F and roast the chicken until browned and the juices at the leg-thigh joint run clear, 1 hour to 1 hour and 15 minutes (a digital thermometer inserted into the thickest part of the thigh should read between 160°F and 165°F). Remove the chicken from the oven and transfer to a cutting board. Tent the chicken loosely with aluminum foil and let the chicken rest for 5 minutes, and then remove the stuffing from the cavity and discard everything but the lemon. Squeeze the lemon halves over the chicken, then carve and serve.

SERVES 4

1 2½- to 3-pound chicken

3 tablespoons unsalted butter, at room temperature

1 fresh sage sprig plus 6 fresh sage leaves

3 tablespoons olive oil

1 tablespoon kosher salt

2 yellow onions, sliced into ½-inch-thick rings, plus 1 yellow onion, quartered

3 fresh thyme sprigs

1 lemon, halved

5 garlic cloves

tip
After taking the chicken out of the oven, place it on your cutting board breast side down so some of the juices collect in the breast, yielding nice moist white meat.

CIDER-SAGE PORK CHOPS

¼ cup canola or grapeseed oil

2 tablespoons kosher salt

4 2-inch-thick double-cut pork chops

4 tablespoons (½ stick) unsalted butter

2 shallots, finely chopped

2 tablespoons finely chopped fresh sage

¼ cup apple cider or apple juice

4 teaspoons cider vinegar

VINNY: Pork is my favorite protein, both for its flavor and for its versatility. There are so many great cuts, and it's relatively inexpensive. Instead of making this with the sage, apple cider, and vinegar, you could use maple syrup, barbecue sauce, or even a dry rub.

Jon: My parents keep a kosher kitchen, and while I respect their traditions, I love the pig and can't imagine a life without bacon. (Sorry, Mom and Dad.) I feel bad that they are missing out on this amazing dish.

PLACE a roasting pan on your oven's middle rack and preheat your oven to 450°F.

Use half of the oil and all of the salt to season all sides of the pork chops. Place the remaining 2 tablespoons of oil in the roasting pan and add the chops. Roast until the edges are crispy-browned, 15 to 18 minutes for medium doneness, turning the chops midway through cooking. (Use a paring knife to make a small slit in the center of a chop to check the doneness.) Spoon some of the pan juices over the chops just before they're done.

Transfer the chops to a cutting board, loosely cover with aluminum foil, and set aside to rest while you make the sauce. Add the butter to the hot roasting pan, and once melted add the shallots and let them sizzle for 15 seconds (if they don't sizzle, return the pan to the oven for 1 minute), and then add the sage, cider, and vinegar.

Serve the chops whole, with the pan juices. Or cut the meat off of the bone, cut it crosswise into ¼-inch strips, divide it among 4 plates, and spoon the sauce over the meat. Serve immediately.

SERVES 4

Chile-Rubbed PORK LOIN

VINNY: I created this recipe when I was back in culinary school; it actually won me a scholarship! It's so good that we still make it when we crave a taste of home. The rub works great on other cuts, too, such as pork chops, chicken breasts, or a flank steak.

Jon: Chili powder, made from dried and ground chiles plus spices such as cumin and oregano, gives the pork a great sweet and smoky taste, while dried ancho chile powder (made from dried poblano chiles) adds a note of fruitiness. If you can't find it, you can use spicy Hungarian paprika or Spanish smoked paprika called *pimentón*.

MIX the spices for the rub in a small bowl. Rub the pork loin with the oil and then evenly pat the spices onto the pork loin. Wrap in plastic wrap and refrigerate for at least 2 hours or overnight.

Preheat your oven to 425°F. Unwrap the roast and place it on a greased rack in your roasting pan. Reduce the oven temperature to 375°F and roast the pork until its internal temperature reaches 150°F, about 45 minutes. Remove from the oven, transfer to a cutting board, and tent the pork loin with aluminum foil. Let the meat sit for 5 to 10 minutes before thinly slicing and serving.

SERVES 4 TO 6

FOR THE RUB

1 tablespoon ancho chile powder
2 teaspoons sweet paprika
1½ teaspoons garlic powder
1½ teaspoons onion powder
2 teaspoons kosher salt
½ teaspoon cayenne pepper
½ teaspoon chili powder

1 2-pound boneless pork loin
2 tablespoons canola or grapeseed oil

+1 pan: strawberry chutney

This chutney is a wonderful complement to the pork loin. Arrowroot gives it a clear and glossy look, but if all you have is cornstarch, that's fine. The chutney will just have a more opaque appearance.

Bring $1/3$ cup granulated sugar, 2 tablespoons brown sugar, and $1/4$ cup balsamic vinegar to a boil in a small nonreactive saucepan. Add 1 cup hulled strawberries and simmer for 3 minutes. Stir in $1/2$ small chopped onion, 1 tablespoon molasses, 1 tablespoon strawberry jam, 1 teaspoon grated ginger, $1/2$ teaspoon chopped garlic, $1/2$ teaspoon cayenne pepper, $1/4$ teaspoon mustard seeds, and $1/4$ teaspoon salt. Simmer until slightly thickened, 20 to 25 minutes.

Stir 1 teaspoon arrowroot powder and 2 teaspons water together in a small dish and add it to the saucepan. Simmer until the chutney is darkened and thicker, about another 30 minutes, and set aside.

Serve warm with the pork loin (or cool to room temperature and refrigerate in an airtight plastic container for up to 5 days).

+1 pan: grits

With pork, shrimp, or even over-easy eggs, grits are totally classic. We like ours on the soft and creamy side. Add 1 cup of any kind of grated cheese at the end to make the grits especially rich, or add bacon or sautéed mushrooms for a little extra flavor.

Bring 3 cups water to a boil in a medium saucepan. Add 1 cup hominy grits and 1 teaspoon kosher salt. Reduce the heat to low and cook, stirring often, until thickened, about 5 minutes. Add 1 cup milk or cream and cook until thick and creamy, about 10 minutes. Stir in 3 tablespoons butter and, once melted, serve. (If using grated cheese, add it with the butter.)

BALSAMIC Barbecued Baby BACKS

FOR THE RIBS

2 racks of pork baby back ribs
   divided in half
Canola or grapeseed oil
4 teaspoons kosher salt
4 fresh flat-leaf parsley sprigs
4 fresh thyme sprigs
4 garlic cloves, smashed

FOR THE BARBECUE SAUCE

1 cup ketchup
1 12-ounce bottle lager-style
   beer (1½ cups)
½ cup balsamic vinegar
1 red onion, diced
1 garlic clove, very finely
   chopped
½ cup packed light brown
   sugar
3 tablespoons honey
1½ tablespoons grainy
   mustard
1 to 2 teaspoons Tabasco
   sauce (depending on how
   tangy you like your ribs)
1 teaspoon Worcestershire
   sauce

VINNY: I'm a fan of smoked ribs, but if you crave a rack and don't have hours and hours to smoke them, these are great. This recipe proves that you can cut corners and still get an end result that's fall-off-the-bone good.

Jon: Wrapping ribs in foil steams them so they stay moist and makes them really tender because the steam helps break down the tough tissues in the meat. We finish them off under the broiler with a swipe of our balsamic barbecue sauce. You can also make them ahead of time and finish them on a kettle grill to get a little smoky edge.

PREHEAT your oven to 500°F.

Place each half rack of ribs on a 2-foot-long sheet of foil, shiny side up. Rub each half rack with some oil and sprinkle with the salt, then divide the herbs and garlic among the packets. Wrap the foil around the ribs tightly and place them in a roasting pan. Roast the ribs for 30 minutes, then reduce the oven temperature to 250°F and cook until the ribs are fork-tender, about 1½ hours longer. Remove from the oven and carefully open the foil so the ribs cool enough to handle, 15 to 20 minutes. Turn off the oven.

While the ribs roast, make the barbecue sauce. Whisk all of the sauce ingredients together in a medium saucepan, add ¼ cup water, and bring to a boil over medium-high heat. Reduce the heat to medium-low, keeping the sauce at a bare simmer, and cook until it is thick, at least for 1 hour (we sometimes cook it for up to 3 hours, partially covered, for an intensely deep flavor).

Turn your oven to broil. Liberally brush the meaty side of the ribs with half of the sauce and broil until caramelized, 2 to 3 minutes. (If you don't have a built-in broiling element in your oven, then crank the oven heat to 500°F and roast the ribs until the sauce is hot and bubbling.) Transfer to a platter and serve with the rest of the barbecue sauce on the side.

SERVES **6 TO 8**

CUBAN-STYLE ROAST PORK

2 cups orange juice
   (preferably fresh)
1 cup olive oil
½ cup fresh lemon juice
   (from about 2 lemons)
½ cup fresh lime juice (from
   about 4 limes)
20 garlic cloves, smashed
4 white onions, halved and
   very thinly sliced, plus
   1 white onion sliced into
   ½-inch-thick rings
3 fresh thyme sprigs
2 bay leaves (preferably fresh,
   not dried)
1 tablespoon ground cumin
1½ teaspoons red pepper
   flakes
4 tablespoons kosher salt
1 6- to 8-pound boneless
   pork butt (sometimes
   called a Boston butt),
   trimmed of excess fat and
   tied into a roast
5 limes cut into wedges, for
   serving

Jon: This roasted pork butt is one of my favorite ways to eat pork. It's so tender and packed with flavor. You could do it up traditionally with rice and black beans, mix it with giant butter beans for a Cuban-style cassoulet, or wrap it in a corn tortilla with pickled red onions (page 34) for killer pork tacos.

VINNY: We got turned on to Cuban roast pork while living in Miami. Pork butt doesn't set you back financially, plus it can feed a crowd. We like to make the full recipe, even if just cooking for a few friends; we'll portion out the leftovers and pack them into freezer bags to pull out on a rainy day.

WHISK the orange juice, all but 2 tablespoons of the olive oil, the lemon juice, lime juice, 15 of the garlic cloves, half of the thinly sliced onions, and the thyme, bay leaves, cumin, red pepper flakes, and 2 tablespoons of the salt in a large bowl. Pour into a large plastic bag (try a small garbage bag) and add the pork. Knot to close and place in a large bowl or in one of your refrigerator's vegetable bins to catch any leakage. Marinate for at least 24 hours or up to 3 days.

Preheat your oven to 450°F.

Separate the ½-inch-thick onion rings and place them, along with the remaining 5 garlic cloves, in the bottom of a roasting pan and drizzle with the remaining 2 tablespoons of olive oil. Remove the roast from the bag (discard the marinade), pat it dry, place it on top of the onions and garlic, and rub with the remaining 2 tablespoons of salt.

Reduce the oven temperature to 425°F and roast the pork for 45 minutes. Reduce the oven temperature to 250°F, cover the roasting pan with foil, and roast until the meat is falling apart, 4 to 4½ hours longer.

Shred the pork and serve with the remaining thinly sliced onions and lots of lime wedges.

SERVES 12

+1 pan: mojo

Mojo is like the ketchup of Cuba. It's a vinegary, pungent tabletop condiment that's used on roasted pork, grilled meats, and pan-seared chicken. Drizzle a little over the pork before serving. It's best served within a hour of making.

Heat ¼ cup canola or grapeseed oil with 2 tablespoons finely chopped garlic in a small saucepan over low heat until the garlic is soft and translucent, 8 to 10 minutes. Turn off the heat and cool until it reaches room temperature, then stir in 2 tablespoons fresh lime juice, 1 tablespoon fresh orange juice, 2 teaspoons fresh lemon juice, ½ teaspoon ground cumin, and ¾ teaspoon kosher salt.

ROSEMARY-GARLIC
Marinated LEG *of* LAMB

2 cups dry red wine (such as pinot noir)

½ cup canola or grapeseed oil

Juice of 1 lemon (save the rinds after juicing)

1 tablespoon red wine vinegar

2 tablespoons grainy mustard

1 tablespoon Worcestershire sauce

20 garlic cloves, finely chopped

5 shallots, roughly chopped

2 bay leaves

2 tablespoons finely chopped fresh rosemary

1 tablespoon finely chopped fresh thyme

3 teaspoons kosher salt

1 3½- to 4-pound boneless leg of lamb, tied into a roast

2 tablespoons olive oil

You can't get more traditional than the pairing of lamb, garlic, and rosemary, but it just *works*. Lamb really dries out if it's overcooked. We like to pull our lamb out of the oven and tent it with foil when the interior is still fairly pink. While the lamb rests, the carryover heat finishes the cooking and gives the juices a chance to reabsorb into the meat before you carve it.

PLACE the red wine, canola or grapeseed oil, lemon juice and the squeezed lemon, red wine vinegar, mustard, Worcestershire, garlic, shallots, bay leaves, rosemary, thyme, and 1 teaspoon of the salt in a gallon-size resealable plastic bag. Seal the bag and shake to combine. Add the lamb roast and refrigerate for at least 4 hours or up to 2 days.

About 2 hours before you plan to serve the lamb, remove it from the marinade and brush off any stuck-on herbs or bits of garlic. Place the roast in a roasting pan and let it sit out at room temperature for 45 minutes.

Preheat your oven to 450°F.

Rub the roast with the olive oil and then sprinkle it with the remaining 2 teaspoons of salt. Reduce the oven temperature to 425°F and cook the roast until browned, about 45 minutes. (If you have a thin roasting pan, place it on a sheet pan so the meat doesn't get too dark on the bottom.) Turn the roast over and cook until it is very browned and its internal temperature reaches 130°F to 135°F on an instant-read thermometer, 15 to 20 minutes more. Remove the lamb from the oven, tent with foil, and let it rest for 15 minutes before slicing thin and serving.

SERVES 8

HARISSA-RUBBED Rack of Lamb with MINT YOGURT

FOR THE HARISSA

1 cup canned tomato purée (no added spices or tomato paste)

6 garlic cloves, very finely chopped

2 tablespoons extra-virgin olive oil

2 teaspoons cayenne pepper

1 teaspoon ground cumin

½ teaspoon ground coriander

3 teaspoons kosher salt

2 1-pound racks of lamb (about 8 ribs each)

FOR THE MINT YOGURT

2 cups plain yogurt

2 tablespoons finely chopped fresh mint

Pinch of kosher salt

> **tip**
> We serve this dish medium rare so it's nice and pink in the middle. (You can make a small slit with a paring knife in the fleshy side of the lamb to check the inside color; keep in mind that it will be pinker in the center.)

Jon: This is our most-requested lamb dish, and it's perfect for people who are on the fence when it comes to lamb.

VINNY: When we have the option, we'll go for Colorado lamb over New Zealand lamb. Colorado chops are bigger and less intensly gamey, but they're pricier, too. Keep in mind that a small New Zealand rack will cook more quickly than an American one.

Jon: Heads up—the lamb needs to sit with the spice paste overnight before cooking, so plan accordingly.

WHISK the tomato purée, garlic, oil, cayenne, cumin, coriander, and 1 teaspoon of the salt together in a small bowl. Rub the paste all over the lamb and then tightly seal the racks in plastic wrap. Place on a plate or in a resealable plastic bag and refrigerate for 6 hours or overnight.

While the meat marinates, stir the yogurt, mint, and salt together in a small bowl. Cover with plastic wrap and refrigerate until serving.

Preheat your oven to 450°F.

Unwrap the lamb, wipe off the excess marinade, and place the racks on their sides in a roasting pan. Sprinkle the racks with the remaining 2 teaspoons of salt. Reduce the oven temperature to 425°F and roast the lamb until it is browned, turning it over midway through cooking, for a total of 9 to 10 minutes for medium-rare.

Transfer the rack to a cutting board, loosely cover with aluminum foil, and let it rest for 5 to 10 minutes before slicing into two-rib chops. Serve with the chilled mint yogurt on the side.

SERVES 4

LONDON BROIL *with* HERB BUTTER

VINNY: There are two ways to see how rare your steak is: cut into it to check its color or stab it with a digital instant-read thermometer and take its temperature. For a rare steak, pull it out when it's around 120°F (the temperature will rise a couple of degrees while it rests), for medium-rare pull it out around 128°F, and for medium around 135°F.

Jon: "London broil" is a generic name for a flat, boneless steak that comes from the top round. It's kind of confusing because sometimes grocery stores have them labeled as a London broil steak, and sometimes they don't. The top round is the most economical London broil option, but other cuts, such as flank and sirloin steaks, work also.

1 2½- to 3-pound top-round London broil (or flank or sirloin steak)
1½ tablespoons canola or grapeseed oil
2 teaspoons kosher salt
2 tablespoons unsalted butter
1 shallot, finely diced
2 garlic cloves, thinly sliced
2 teaspoons chopped fresh flat-leaf parsley
½ teaspoon finely chopped fresh thyme
Juice of 1 lemon

PLACE a roasting pan on the middle rack and preheat your oven to 450°F.

Season all sides of the steak with half of the oil and 1½ teaspoons of the salt. Add the remaining oil to the roasting pan and place the steak in the pan. Roast the steak for 14 to 16 minutes (for medium-rare; use a paring knife to make a small slit in the thickest part of the steak to check for doneness), turning the steak over midway through cooking and spooning some of the pan juices over the steak just before it is done.

Transfer the steak to a cutting board, tent with foil, and set aside to rest while you make the sauce. Add the butter to the roasting pan, and once melted add the shallots and let them sizzle for 15 seconds (if they don't sizzle, return the pan to the oven for 1 minute). Add the garlic, parsley, thyme, lemon juice, and remaining ½ teaspoon of salt to the pan and stir to combine. Thinly slice the steak against the grain. Arrange on a platter or divide it among 6 plates and spoon the herb butter over it. Serve immediately.

SERVES 6

GARLIC-HERB Crusted PRIME RIB *with* MADEIRA SAUCE

FOR THE PRIME RIB

½ cup finely chopped fresh flat-leaf parsley

¼ cup finely chopped fresh chives

3 tablespoons finely chopped garlic

2 tablespoons finely chopped fresh thyme

1 5- to 6-pound boneless rib-eye roast

2 tablespoons kosher salt

3 to 4 tablespoons olive oil

FOR THE SAUCE

1½ cups Madeira

2 tablespoons fresh lemon juice

1 shallot, finely chopped

1 garlic clove, finely chopped

1 tablespoon tomato paste

3 fresh thyme sprigs

3 whole black peppercorns

½ bay leaf

2 tablespoons heavy cream

1 cup (2 sticks) unsalted butter, cold and cut into ½-inch pieces

1½ teaspoons kosher salt

This roast definitely makes a statement: it's the ultimate holiday cut because it makes everyone happy. Those who like their meat on the medium-well side can have the ends, and the interior slices are served to those who like it pink.

PREHEAT your oven to 450°F and adjust the oven rack to the lower-middle position. Mix the parsley, chives, garlic, and thyme together in a small bowl. Rub the roast all over with the salt and then rub on 3 tablespoons of the olive oil. Pat on the herbs and place the roast in a roasting pan.

Reduce the oven temperature to 425°F and cook the roast to your preferred degree of doneness, 1 hour for rare to medium-rare, 1 hour and 15 minutes for medium-rare to medium, and 1 hour and 30 minutes for medium. (Note that a medium roast will have pretty well-done ends and will be medium in the center.)

While the beef roasts, whisk the Madeira, lemon juice, shallots, garlic, tomato paste, thyme, peppercorns, and bay leaf together in a large saucepan. Bring to a simmer over medium-high heat, reduce the heat to medium-low, and cook until only ¼ cup of liquid is left in the pan, 10 to 12 minutes. Stir in the cream and cook until it has reduced by half, 2 to 3 minutes. Whisk in the cold butter a few tablespoons at a time and then stir in the salt. Turn off the heat and cover with plastic wrap to keep warm until serving.

Remove the roast from the oven and place it on a cutting board. Tent with foil and let it rest for 15 minutes, then slice thin and serve with the warm Madeira sauce.

SERVES 8 TO 10

Bacon-Wrapped MEATLOAF

Jon: My mom's meatloaf was so bad that it turned me off of meatloaf for a long time. Then Vin was like "dude, meatloaf is great!" He was right; his take on the loaf opened my eyes, and now I'm the one making meatloaf all the time!

VINNY: Adding bread crumbs and milk directly to the meat mixture is a shortcut we take instead of soaking slices of bread in milk. The bread crumbs integrate better into the mixture this way, too.

PREHEAT your oven to 350°F. Line a roasting pan with aluminum foil and set aside.

Place all of the ingredients except for the bacon in a large bowl and mix with your hands until thoroughly combined.

Lay a 16 by 12-inch piece of plastic wrap lengthwise on your work surface and arrange the bacon strips vertically on the plastic, slightly overlapping. Turn the meat out on top of the bacon and form into a loaf shape with your hands by pressing the loaf lengthwise along the bacon first, and then shaping the sides.

Use the sides of the plastic to wrap and press the bacon around the loaf. Transfer the loaf to the prepared pan and flip it over. Gently remove the plastic wrap. Bake until the meatloaf is firm to the touch and the bacon starts to brown, about 50 to 60 minutes (for extra-crisp bacon, place the meatloaf under your broiler for 2 to 3 minutes). Set aside for 10 minutes to cool before slicing (a serrated knife works the best for slicing through the bacon) and serving.

SERVES 8 TO 10

1½ pounds ground chuck
1½ pounds ground pork
1 Spanish onion, diced
¾ cup panko bread crumbs (see Note, page 79)
2 large eggs
1 cup ketchup
⅓ cup milk
½ cup finely chopped fresh flat-leaf parsley
2 garlic cloves, very finely chopped
1 tablespoon Worcestershire sauce
½ teaspoon Tabasco sauce
2 teaspoons kosher salt
1 teaspoon cayenne pepper
8 thick bacon slices

ROASTED BONES *with* Parsley, Toast, *and* Aged BALSAMIC

VINNY: Marrow is like meaty butter, and it is definitely one of my favorite things to eat. Whoever discovered roasting bones, digging out the marrow, and spreading it on brioche is a genius.

Jon: Whenever we're in New York City we always go to Blue Ribbon and order their marrow bones. It's not something you make a meal of, but there's nothing better than a little marrow on toast to start a weekend off right.

PREHEAT your oven to 500°F and line a roasting pan with parchment paper. Place the bones cut side down on the pan and roast until the bones start to color and the marrow inside is soft and doesn't resist slight pressure, 20 to 25 minutes.

Scoop out the marrow and spread it onto the toast. Sprinkle with the salt and parsley, drizzle with balsamic, and serve.

SERVES 8

8 2-inch-long center-cut beef or veal marrow bones

8 slices brioche bread, toasted and halved diagonally

1 teaspoon kosher salt

½ cup whole fresh flat-leaf parsley leaves

Aged balsamic vinegar for serving (or balsamic reduction; see Note)

---

fake it

If you don't have any hundred-year-old balsamic hanging out in the house, you can get kind of the same effect by making a balsamic reduction with the cheap stuff from the grocery story. Place 1 cup balsamic vinegar in a small saucepan over low heat (you don't want to see any bubbles at all) and cook until it is reduced to 2 tablespoons, about 1 hour. Be sure to reduce it over the lowest heat your stovetop can muster, otherwise the balsamic can take on a bitter flavor.

BAKING
DISH

Jon: Most of the time, I don't have much of a sweet tooth, so Vin is better at coming up with desserts. That said, I have no problem attacking the fridge late at night for a sugar hit! I love eating dessert straight from the fridge; I'll spoon the hell out of a good tiramisù!

VINNY: I've always had a sweet tooth. My dad baked a lot for me while I was growing up. I guess I inherited my love for pastry from him.

Jon: Desserts can be as simple or complicated as you want to make them. But one thing I've learned is that people who like dessert are often just as happy with an easy-to-make chocolate cake as they are with a tricked-out one with lots of components and drizzles and fruit sauces. Do you really need to make a high-maintenance tart when some of your buds are coming over to hang out?

VINNY: We find that our friends are just as happy with my grandma's cornflake bars (see page 223) as they are with some high-end and manipulated dessert. That's why we like to keep our desserts on the rustic, homey side. Like upside-down cake, bread pudding, crisps, and bar cookies. These are the desserts that people really get into—the stuff they grew up with as kids.

Jon: When we thought back to what we ate for dessert as kids, it seemed like every one of them came out of the standard rectangular glass Pyrex dish! I swear, it's one of the most versatile baking dishes ever created.

VINNY: Ceramic pie dishes, springform pans, Bundt pans, trifle dishes, and the like are all nice to accumulate over the years. But when it comes down to it, all you really need is that inexpensive nine by thirteen-inch (three-quart) glass baking dish and you're golden. Fancy bakeware isn't a necessity.

Jon: We should know. You won't find one ceramic-glazed porcelain whatever in our kitchen! We'd probably break it after the first go-around.

VINNY: People always seem to stress out over desserts. So we've tried to keep them pretty simple to encourage you to make them more often. Who knows, maybe I'll even get Jon to make dessert one of these days!

Jon: You make them, and I'll eat them. That's how I like my dessert.

MENU

WHATEVER Upside-Down **CAKE**

Tender **BISCUITS**

SOUR CREAM Coffee Cake *with* **CINNAMON-PECAN** Streusel

Chocolate-Hazelnut **BREAD PUDDING**

LAVENDER–LEMON BARS

VINNY'S *Grandma's* **Coconut-Almond-Cornflake BARS**

PUMPKIN PIE Bars

Pistachio TIRAMISÙ

STRAWBERRY-RHUBARB Crisp

Fallen **CHOCOLATE** Cake

WHATEVER Upside-Down CAKE

1 cup (2 sticks) plus
   1 tablespoon unsalted
   butter, at room
   temperature
1 cup light brown sugar
1¾ pounds fruit, thinly sliced
   (about 5½ cups peeled
   apples, fresh figs, mangos,
   peeled pears, or plums)
2 cups all-purpose flour
¼ cup cornmeal
2 teaspoons baking powder
½ teaspoon salt
1 cup plus 2 tablespoons
   whole milk
2 teaspoons vanilla extract
6 large eggs, separated
1½ cups plus 1½ tablespoons
   granulated sugar

VINNY: We made the classic pineapple version of upside-down cake when we catered the VIP tent for Tony Hawk's Boom Boom Huck Jam, a tour that features top skateboarders, BMXers, and freestyle Moto-X bikers. In the summer, this is gorgeous with fuchsia-colored plums. In the fall we make it with fresh figs.

Jon: We always try to use fruit that is in season. It makes sense for us from a business perspective because out-of-season produce usually costs an arm and a leg. I love it when Vin makes this cake: the sweet burnt-sugar smell of the caramel cooking is insane.

PREHEAT your oven to 350°F. Grease a 9 by 13-inch baking dish with the 1 tablespoon of softened butter and set aside.

Melt 6 tablespoons of the butter in a heatproof bowl in the microwave. Add the brown sugar and cook in 30-second increments until dissolved, stirring often, 3 to 4 minutes. Pour the hot mixture into the prepared baking dish. Add the sliced fruit, arranging it in vertical rows, and set aside.

Whisk the flour, cornmeal, baking powder, and salt together in a large bowl or on a sheet of wax paper and set aside. Combine the milk and vanilla in a liquid measuring cup and set aside.

Using an electric mixer or beaters or a whisk, whip the egg whites on high speed in a large bowl until foamy. Slowly sprinkle in the 1½ tablespoons of granulated sugar, whipping until the egg whites hold medium peaks. When you dip into the egg whites with a spoon and pull it out, a peak with a curved tip should form. (If you are using a stand mixer and don't have a second bowl, gently transfer the whites to another bowl and wipe out the mixer bowl.)

With the mixer, cream the remaining 10 tablespoons of butter with the remaining 1½ cups of sugar on medium speed until pale yellow and fluffy, 2 to 3 minutes. Add the egg yolks one at a time, mixing thoroughly after each addition and scraping down the bowl as necessary. With the mixer running on low speed, alternate adding the flour mixture and the milk mixture, beginning with one third of the flour, following with half of the milk, adding half of the remaining flour, the rest of the milk, and ending with the remaining flour, scraping down the mixer bowl as necessary. Gently fold in half of the egg whites using a rubber spatula until nearly incorporated. Add the remaining whipped egg whites, folding in until just incorporated.

Gently transfer the batter to the baking dish, spreading it evenly over the fruit. Bake until the cake is golden and springs back from light pressure, 50 to 60 minutes. Cool in the pan for 10 minutes and then run a paring knife around the edges of the cake. Place a serving platter on top of the cake and flip the baking dish over, gently shaking the pan to release the cake onto the platter. Slice the cake into 9 equal squares and serve solo or with Spiked Anglaise.

SERVES 8 TO 10

folding egg whites

Folding whipped egg whites into batter isn't hard, it just requires a delicate touch. Hold a rubber spatula perpendicular to the middle of the whipped egg whites and submerge it until you hit the bottom of the bowl. Run the spatula from the bottom up along the side of the bowl. Give the bowl a quarter turn and repeat. The goal is to fold the egg whites in without losing all of the fragile air pockets you just whipped into them. With patience and practice, you'll be folding like a pro.

+ 1 pan: spiked anglaise

This classic vanilla sauce is great with this upside-down cake, with our flourless chocolate cake (see page 231)—even with pumpkin bars (see page 224). We add a little liqueur for a kick; try Frangelico, rum, Grand Marnier, or brandy.

Bring 2 cups heavy cream, ½ cup sugar, and half of a split vanilla bean to a simmer in a large saucepan over medium-high heat. Meanwhile, place 5 egg yolks and ¼ cup sugar in a large bowl and whisk to combine. While whisking, slowly drizzle the cream mixture into the eggs until the bottom of the bowl is warm.

Return the egg mixture to the saucepan and place over medium heat. While stirring constantly, cook the mixture until it begins to steam (but isn't boiling) and becomes thick, 8 to 10 minutes. You can tell it's right when you dip a spoon into the sauce and draw your finger across the back of the spoon; it should leave a clear trail. (If the mixture looks lumpy, strain it through a fine-mesh sieve.) Stir in 2 tablespoons of liqueur. Cool completely and refrigerate (this can be made up to 2 days in advance). Remove the vanilla bean before serving.

Tender BISCUITS

Jon: Growing up in Florida, I used to ride my bike to this place called Patch's for breakfast and get their sausage and biscuits. Even now, I really can't control myself around a platter of good fluffy biscuits.

VINNY: Don't stress it if your biscuits aren't perfect looking. To me, biscuits aren't about refinement. I like how each one looks a little different from the others, you know?

PREHEAT your oven to 350°F.

In a large bowl whisk together the flour, sugar, baking powder, and salt. Add the butter and work it into the flour with your fingertips until the mixture looks like a coarse meal and no butter pieces are bigger than a small pea. Drizzle in the cup of cream, working it in with your fingertips until the dough comes together.

Flour your work surface to prevent the dough from sticking. Roll or pat the dough into a 12-inch-long and 5-inch-wide rectangle that is about ½ inch thick. Cut the dough in half horizontally to make two long strips, then cut the dough vertically to make 10 square biscuits. Place the biscuits in a 9 by 13-inch baking dish and brush with the remaining 3 tablespoons of cream.

Recipe Continues . . .

2 cups plus 2 tablespoons all-purpose flour, plus extra for rolling

¼ cup sugar

1½ tablespoons baking powder

¼ teaspoon kosher salt

4 tablespoons (½ stick) cold unsalted butter, cut into small pieces

1 cup cold heavy cream, plus 3 tablespoons for brushing

---

salvaging burnt gravy
You need to be diligent about stirring the gravy while it cooks so it doesn't burn. But if a film of the gravy does get scorched on the bottom of the pot, it's an easy fix. Just scoop up the top layer and leave the burnt stuff behind.

Bake the biscuits until they are tall and just starting to color, about 10 minutes. Rotate the pan and continue to bake until the tops are golden, another 8 to 10 minutes. Remove from the oven and transfer to a wire rack to cool (the biscuits are best eaten within 2 hours of baking).

MAKES 10 BISCUITS

+1 pan: jimmy jon's sausage gravy

Melt 4 tablespoons ($\frac{1}{2}$ stick) unsalted butter in a large pot or skillet over medium-high heat. Crumble one 16-ounce tube of Jimmy Dean's fresh breakfast sausage into the pot and cook, stirring often, until browned, about 5 to 7 minutes. Mix in $\frac{1}{3}$ cup all-purpose flour and cook, stirring constantly, until the flour becomes a pale brown color, 3 to 4 minutes. Stir in $2\frac{3}{4}$ cups heavy cream, a little at a time at first to make a paste, and then slowly incorporate the remaining cream. Cook until the sauce is slightly thick, stirring slowly, about 5 minutes. Mix in $\frac{1}{4}$ cup maple syrup, 2 teaspoons Tabasco sauce, some freshly ground black pepper, and salt if necessary. Serve hot over split biscuits.

SOUR CREAM Coffee Cake *with* CINNAMON-PECAN STREUSEL

VINNY: Coffee cake always makes me think of chill weekend brunches. It's a really nice treat, and it's easy to make; there's no downside.

Jon: We make big batches of the streusel and freeze it so we can make this coffee cake at the drop of a hat. The streusel even works with a fruit crisp. I like it on ice cream, too.

PREHEAT your oven to 350°F.

To make the streusel, stir the sugar, flour, cinnamon, and salt in a bowl. Add the butter and mix in using a fork so you get knobby chunks. Mix in the pecans and set aside.

Grease a 9 by 13-inch baking dish with the 2 tablespoons of butter and then dust with the 2 tablespoons of flour. Set aside. In a large bowl, whisk together the remaining 2 cups of flour, the baking powder, baking soda, and salt. Whisk the eggs, 2 tablespoons water, and the vanilla together in a small bowl and set aside.

Using an electric mixer or beater or a wooden spoon, cream the remaining 1½ sticks of butter with the sugar until pale yellow and fluffy, 2 to 3 minutes. Add the sour cream in two additions, mixing thoroughly after each and scraping down the bowl as necessary. Add one third of the dry ingredients and follow with half of the liquid ingredients, mixing until just nearly incorporated and scraping down the bowl as necessary. Add half of the remaining dry mixture followed by the remaining liquid ingredients and ending with the rest of the dry mixture, scraping down the bowl as necessary.

Recipe Continues . . .

FOR THE STREUSEL

1 cup sugar

½ cup all-purpose flour

1½ tablespoons ground cinnamon

½ teaspoon salt

4 tablespoons (½ stick) unsalted butter, melted

1½ cups pecan halves, roughly chopped

FOR THE CAKE

¾ cup plus 2 tablespoons (1¾ sticks) unsalted butter, at room temperature

2 cups plus 2 tablespoons all-purpose flour

1½ teaspoons baking powder

¼ teaspoon baking soda

½ teaspoon salt

3 large eggs

2 teaspoons vanilla extract

1 cup granulated sugar

1 cup sour cream

Confectioners' sugar, for serving

Transfer half of the batter to the baking dish and spread it evenly. Sprinkle with half of the streusel and cover with the remaining batter. Top with the rest of the streusel. Bake until a toothpick or wooden skewer inserted into the center of the cake comes out dry, 35 to 40 minutes. Eat warm or cool completely before cutting into squares. Dust with confectioners' sugar before serving.

SERVES **8** TO **10**

+1 pan: rum caramel sauce

Caramel sauce adds an element of fanciness to the most basic stuff, such as a scoop of vanilla ice cream or fresh strawberries. It puts this coffee cake over the top.

Place 2 cups plus 3 tablespoons sugar in a medium saucepan over medium-high heat. Once the sugar melts, reduce the heat to medium and cook the sugar until it's deep amber, 3 to 6 minutes, swirling the pan often to keep the sugar from burning (be careful: molten sugar is really hot!). Turn off the heat and add 3 cups plus 2 tablespoons warmed heavy cream (the sugar will bubble up initially) and whisk until smooth. Whisk in 2 tablespoons rum. Serve warm or at room temperature. Store in a plastic container in the refrigerator for up to 2 weeks and reheat in the microwave or in a saucepan over low heat.

CHOCOLATE-HAZELNUT Bread Pudding

5¾ cups half-and-half, heavy cream, or buttermilk

4 large egg yolks

4 large eggs

1 cup sugar

1 tablespoon ground cinnamon

6 to 7 cups cubed crustless day-old bread (we like French bread)

12 ounces gianduja (hazelnut-flavored chocolate) or 65% to 70% cacao chocolate, finely chopped (see Note)

---

tip

Day-old bread is best for bread pudding, but if you didn't plan ahead, toast fresh bread in a 250°F oven until it's dry on the outside and still gives in the middle.

Jon: Bread pudding is genius, because when I screw up and buy too much bread for a party, it covers my tracks! The coolest thing is that it works best with one- or two-day-old bread, and we hate being wasteful.

VINNY: Unlike some bread puddings that are firm enough to serve in squares, we make ours on the loose side, more pudding than bread. If you prefer it more solid, bake it a little longer. For a super-rich dessert, use heavy cream, and for a Southern twist, go for tangy buttermilk.

PREHEAT your oven to 350°F.

Whisk the half-and-half (or cream or buttermilk), egg yolks, eggs, sugar, and cinnamon together in a large bowl. Add the bread cubes and push them down into the liquid to soak them all the way through. Set the mixture aside for 10 minutes.

Use your hands to scoop half of the bread cubes out of the mixing bowl and spread them in a 9 by 13-inch baking dish. Sprinkle the bread layer with all but 2 tablespoons of the chocolate. Cover with the remaining bread cubes and pour in as much of the liquid as you can without overflowing the baking dish. Top with the remaining chocolate. Bake until the edges are puffy and light golden brown and the center is dry to the touch, 1 hour to 1 hour and 15 minutes. Serve warm or cool completely before serving in bowls.

SERVES 8 TO 10

---

high cacao

Chocolate is made of two things: cacao and everything else. The higher the percentage of cacao, the more intense and bitter the chocolate will be because there is less sugar, vanilla, and other ingredients added. In this recipe, we want a smooth and intense but not bitter chocolate flavor, so we go with 65 to 70 percent cacao chocolate.

Lavender-LEMON BARS

Jon: This is a standby for us because you can bake the bars en masse and they transport easily. I can't even count how many thousands of lemon bars I've made over the past few years. If lavender isn't your thing, then leave it out and use chopped fresh thyme or lemon zest instead. If you have access to fresh lavender, by all means use it instead of the dried.

VINNY: These bars are intense. The lavender crust is delicate and buttery and the lemon curd on top is really rich and tart. Red, ripe strawberries are my favorite garnish for them. When strawberries hit the farmer's markets in May and June, I swear, they're so juicy and sweet that I can smell them from a block away.

PREHEAT your oven to 325°F. Grease a 9 by 13-inch baking dish with the 1 tablespoon of butter and set aside.

To make the crust, place the flour, confectioners' sugar, salt, and dried lavender in a large bowl and stir to combine. Add the remaining ¾ cup of butter and work in with your fingertips until the mixture looks like a coarse meal, with no butter pieces larger than a small pea. (If you have a food processor, you can make the crust in it: pulse the butter into the flour mixture until it looks like a coarse meal and proceed with the recipe.) Transfer the mixture to the prepared baking dish and press firmly into an even layer. Bake until the crust is just starting to color, 20 to 25 minutes, and set aside to cool completely.

Whisk the eggs, granulated sugar, and flour in a large bowl. Mix in the lemon zest and juice and pour the filling over the baked crust. Bake until the custard is completely set with only a slight jiggle when you shake the pan, 25 to 30 minutes. Let the bars cool completely and then refrigerate.

Recipe Continues . . .

FOR THE CRUST

¾ cup (1½ sticks) plus 1 tablespoon cold unsalted butter, cut into small pieces
1½ cups all-purpose flour
½ cup confectioners' sugar, plus extra for serving
¼ teaspoon salt
2 tablespoons dried lavender

FOR THE FILLING

6 large eggs
1½ cups granulated sugar
½ cup all-purpose flour
Finely grated zest of 3 lemons
1 cup plus 2 tablespoons fresh lemon juice (from 5 to 6 lemons)

To serve, cut into 4 rows across by 3 rows lengthwise, then sprinkle with confectioners' sugar. (Store in an airtight plastic container and in layers separated by parchment or wax paper for up to 3 days.)

MAKES 12 BARS

---

tips

Place a lemon bar on a plate and top with some sliced strawberries and you've got a pretty fancy dessert. Two pints of super-ripe strawberries are all you'll need. If they're less than juicy-ripe and dripping with sugar, slice them and toss with a tablespoon of sugar and a squeeze of lemon juice. Let them sit for 30 minutes before serving.

A Microplane grater is the best tool for grating the lemon zest into very fine bits.

. . . VARIATION

KEY LIME BARS

Follow the instructions on page 224 for making and baking the graham cracker crust. Meanwhile, whisk together 12 large egg yolks, 2 14-ounce cans of sweetened condensed milk, and 1½ cups of key lime juice (fresh or bottled, or if you can't find key lime juice, use regular fresh lime juice). Pour the filling into the baked and cooled crust and bake at 375°F until the filling is set around the edges and the center springs back to very light pressure and jiggles only slightly when tapped, 18 to 25 minutes. Set aside to cool and then refrigerate until cold. Follow the serving instructions above.

Vinny's Grandma's COCONUT-ALMOND-CORNFLAKE Bars

Jon: Vin makes these bars for us to have around the house. They're even better than Rice Krispies treats!

VINNY: We're not the only ones who love them, either: the few times we have served these at parties, people have gone crazy for them. They're kind of like a macaroon, but better than any macaroon you've ever tasted! Because they're cereal-based, they really don't stay fresh for more than one day—not that they would last that long, anyway!

HEAT your oven to 350°F. Place the almonds in a 9 by 13-inch baking dish and roast until they're fragrant and just starting to brown, about 4 minutes. Stir, then add the coconut and bake until the coconut becomes golden and fragrant and the almonds are a deeper brown, another 4 to 6 minutes. Transfer to a bowl to cool.

Place the butter in the baking dish and set in the oven. Once the butter is melted, stir in the marshmallows and bake, stirring occasionally, until completely melted, 4 to 6 minutes. Stir in the toasted coconut and almonds and the cornflakes and refrigerate. Once set, slice into 1½- to 2-inch squares and serve (store in the refrigerator for up to 1 day).

MAKES 2 DOZEN 1½- TO 2-INCH SQUARES

1 cup sliced almonds

2 cups sweetened shredded coconut

10 tablespoons (1 stick plus 2 tablespoons) unsalted butter, cut into 1-inch pieces

8 cups mini marshmallows

8 cups cornflakes

+1 pan: chocolate-frosted bars

Place 8 ounces finely chopped bittersweet chocolate (2 cups) in a small bowl. Heat ¼ cup heavy cream in a small saucepan until it comes to a simmer. Pour the cream over the chocolate and cover the bowl with plastic wrap. Set aside for 5 minutes, and then stir to incorporate. Spread the ganache over the unsliced bars and refrigerate until set. Slice into squares and serve the same day.

PUMPKIN Pie BARS

FOR THE CRUST

1½ cups graham cracker
  crumbs (see Tip)
½ cup sugar
6 tablespoons (¾ stick)
  unsalted butter, melted

FOR THE FILLING

1½ 15-ounce cans pumpkin
  purée (2¾ cups)
1 cup sugar
2¼ teaspoons ground ginger
1½ teaspoons ground nutmeg
  (preferably freshly ground
  or grated)
¾ teaspoon salt
1½ 14-ounce cans sweetened
  condensed milk (2⅓ cups)
3 large eggs, lightly beaten

Sweetened whipped cream,
  for serving

If you feel like roasting your own pumpkins, go for it, but it's definitely not necessary. We've done it, but honestly, once you add the spices and condensed milk, you can't detect much of a difference between fresh roasted pumpkin and the canned pumpkin purée. Just be sure not to buy canned pumpkin pie filling by mistake, because it contains spices and other ingredients.

PREHEAT your oven to 375°F.

To make the crust, in a large bowl combine the graham cracker crumbs and sugar. Stir in the butter and press the mixture evenly into a 9 by 13-inch baking dish. Bake until the crust is just starting to brown and smells toasty, 8 to 10 minutes. Remove from the oven and set aside to cool.

Meanwhile, make the filling. Whisk together the pumpkin purée, sugar, ginger, nutmeg, and salt, then add the condensed milk and eggs and beat to combine. Pour over the cooled crust and bake until puffy around the edges and the center does not jiggle when tapped, 40 to 50 minutes. Cool completely before slicing into squares and serving with whipped cream.

MAKES 16 BARS

> ### tip
> When it comes to making graham cracker crumbs, you have options. If you have a food processor, grinding the crackers in it is probably the fastest and easiest method. Otherwise you can make crumbs by placing the crackers in a gallon-size resealable plastic bag (make sure that there isn't any air trapped in the bag) and using a rolling pin or the bottom of a skillet to smash them into crumbs. It works, and it is a great way to channel your energy!

PISTACHIO Tiramisù

½ cup granulated sugar

¾ cup freshly brewed espresso

2 tablespoons brandy, crème de cacao, or Grand Marnier (optional)

2 cups heavy cream

½ vanilla bean (optional)

1½ teaspoons vanilla extract

2 teaspoons powdered gelatin (about 1 envelope)

½ cup mascarpone or ricotta cheese, at room temperature

24 ladyfinger cookies (about 1 7.1-ounce package)

½ cup chopped toasted pistachios (see page 29)

1 tablespoon cocoa powder

1 tablespoon confectioners' sugar

Jon: One of the best things about hotels is room service, and there's almost nothing better than falling into a king-size bed and having some dessert sent up. If tiramisù is on the menu, that's what I order. Even a hotel restaurant can't mess up tiramisù!

VINNY: This is our cobbled-together quick version of tiramisù. Instead of beating eggs over simmering water to thicken them, we add gelatin and then fold in whipped cream. It's not the most traditional way to make it, but it takes half the time and tastes just as good.

BRING ¼ cup of water and ¼ cup of the granulated sugar to a simmer in a small saucepan. Once the sugar is dissolved, add the espresso and liqueur (if using) and set aside.

Place ½ cup of the cream in a small bowl (keep the remaining 1½ cups in the refrigerator to stay cold). Split the vanilla bean and scrape the seeds into the bowl, then add the bean. Microwave on high power in 30-second increments until the cream comes to a bare simmer. Add the gelatin, and whisk until it dissolves. Let the mixture cool slightly. Remove the vanilla bean.

Using an electric mixer or a whisk, begin to beat the remaining 1½ cups of cream on medium-high speed. Once the mixture becomes frothy, add the gelatin mixture and add the remaining ¼ cup of granulated sugar, sprinkling it in a little at a time and beating just until the cream forms soft peaks. Use a rubber spatula to fold in the mascarpone or ricotta and set aside.

Place an even layer of the ladyfingers about ½ inch apart in a 9 by 13-inch baking dish. Using a pastry brush or a spoon, moisten the ladyfingers with half of the espresso syrup so they are wet but not disintegrating. Spread half of the cheese mixture over the ladyfingers and sprinkle with half of the pistachios. Repeat with another layer of ladyfingers, moisten with the remaining espresso syrup, cover with the rest of the cheese mixture, and sprinkle with the remaining pistachios. Press plastic wrap directly onto the surface of the tiramisù and refrigerate for at least 4 hours.

Whisk together the cocoa powder and confectioners' sugar in a small bowl. Transfer to a sieve and tap gently to dust the top of the tiramisù just before serving.

SERVES 8 TO 10

+1 pan: sweet cherry sauce

To give tiramisù a modern, fresh edge, we like to serve it with stewed cherry sauce.

Place 2 cups pitted Bing or Rainier cherries, ¼ cup water, ½ cup sugar, 1 tablespoon all-purpose flour, 1 split and scraped vanilla bean, 1 teaspoon vanilla extract, and the juice of ½ lemon in a medium saucepan over medium-high heat. Bring to a simmer and reduce the heat to medium. Cook, stirring often, until the cherries break down and the juices are thickened, about 5 to 8 minutes. Cool completely, discard the vanilla bean, and serve.

Strawberry-RHUBARB Crisp

FOR THE CRISP TOPPING

1 cup all-purpose flour

½ cup old-fashioned rolled
  oats (not instant or quick-
  cooking)

½ cup packed light brown
  sugar

½ cup granulated sugar

¼ teaspoon salt

8 tablespoons (1 stick) cold
  unsalted butter, cut into
  small pieces

FOR THE FRUIT

1½ pounds rhubarb, sliced
  into ½-inch pieces

1 pint strawberries, hulled
  and halved

1¼ cups granulated sugar

¼ cup all-purpose flour

Juice of ½ lemon

Vanilla ice cream, for serving

---

tip

Okay, we admit it: we have,
on occasion, used a store-
bought premade pie shell
to make pies on the fly. Just
take one of the fruit fillings
here and load it into a pie
shell. Top with the crisp
topping for a Dutch-style
pie, and bake.

Jon: For fresh-from-the-oven crisp, have the baking dish filled with fruit, topped with streusel, and ready to bake. When you sit down for dinner, place the crisp in your preheated oven. By the time you're clearing away dishes, the crisp is done. Be sure to set a timer just in case you're having a good time and forget that dessert is in the oven!

VINNY: The more often you open the door to check on the crisp, the longer it will take the fruit to cook (and the soggier the topping will become). Instead of messing with the oven door, learn to love your oven light.

PREHEAT your oven to 375°F.

To make the topping, whisk the flour, oats, sugars, and salt together in a large bowl. Add the butter and work it in with your fingertips until the mixture looks like a coarse meal, with no butter pieces bigger than a large pea. Refrigerate for at least 30 minutes (the crisp topping can be made up to 3 days in advance, or it can be frozen to use within a couple of months).

Place the rhubarb, strawberries, sugar, and flour in a 9 by 13-inch baking dish and toss with your hands to evenly distribute the dry ingredients. Add the lemon juice and toss to combine. Cover the fruit with the crisp topping and set the crisp on the middle rack in your oven (place a baking sheet on the lowest rack to catch any potential spillage). Bake, rotating midway through, until the topping is golden brown and the fruit juices bubble up around the edges, about 35 minutes. Serve with a scoop of ice cream.

SERVES 8 TO 10

... VARIATIONS

PEACH-BLUEBERRY CRISP

Follow the instructions for the Strawberry-Rhubarb Crisp, substituting 2 pounds peeled, halved, pitted, and thinly sliced peaches and 1 pint blueberries for the strawberries and rhubarb. Reduce the amount of sugar added to the fruit to ⅔ or ¾ cup, depending on how sweet your peaches are.

CINNAMON-APPLE CRISP

Place 2 tablespoons unsalted butter, 2 pounds peeled, cored, and thinly sliced Granny Smith apples, ¾ cup sugar, ¼ cup all-purpose flour, and 2 teaspoons ground cinnamon next to your cooktop. Melt 1 tablespoon of the butter in a large skillet over medium-high heat. Add half of the apples and brown for 1 minute, then stir in half of the sugar and cook, stirring often, until the apples just start to turn golden brown, about 3 minutes. Stir in half of the flour and half of the cinnamon and cook until the mixture is thick but not dry, stirring often, about 2 more minutes, and transfer to a 9 by 13-inch baking dish. Repeat with the remaining butter, apples, sugar, flour, and cinnamon. Sprinkle the apples in the baking dish with the juice from ½ lemon. Evenly cover with the crisp topping and proceed with baking the crisp as instructed.

FRUIT COBBLER

Whip up the biscuit dough on page 213. Brush the tops of the biscuits with a little cream and sprinkle with some coarse sugar before arranging them over one of the fruit fillings above, in place of the crisp topping. Bake according to the recipe instructions.

Fallen CHOCOLATE Cake

VINNY: This is one of our most requested desserts. It's an awesome cake for all of those no-gluten, no-wheat people (we get a lot of them in L.A.).

Jon: This is really cool served in individual portions. Use ramekins or grease a muffin tin with pan spray.

PREHEAT your oven to 350°F.

Place the butter and the chocolate in a 9 by 13-inch baking dish. Bake until the butter and chocolate have melted. Scrape into a large bowl and whisk together to combine. Wash the baking dish, dry it, grease it with nonstick cooking spray, and set it aside. Whisk into the chocolate mixture 1¼ cups of the sugar, the egg yolks, ¼ cup plus 2 tablespoons water, the vanilla, and the salt. Set aside.

Using an electric mixer or a whisk, beat the egg whites until they are foamy. Slowly sprinkle in the remaining ¼ cup of sugar until the egg whites hold soft peaks (dip into the egg whites with a spoon and pull it out; a soft peak with a very curved tip should form). Gently fold half of the whites into the chocolate mixture until just a few white streaks remain (see page 212 for egg white folding tips). Gently fold in the rest of the egg whites.

Carefully transfer the batter to the prepared baking dish. Bake for 50 to 55 minutes, or until only a couple of crumbs stick to a cake tester inserted into the cake's center. Remove the cake from the oven; if the edges of the cake are hooked over the baking dish, use a rubber spatula to gently ease them toward the center. The cake should fall once it comes out of the oven. Set aside to cool completely. Slice into squares, dust with confectioners' sugar, and serve.

SERVES 8 TO 10

1¼ pounds (4½ sticks) unsalted butter, at room temperature

18 ounces 70% cacao chocolate, finely chopped (see Note, page 218)

Nonstick cooking spray

1½ cups granulated sugar

9 large eggs, separated

1 tablespoon vanilla extract

1 teaspoon sea salt

Confectioners' sugar, for serving

tip
Sprinkle the top of the cake with ½ teaspoon coarse sea salt before baking and serve it with the Rum Caramel Sauce (page 216) for an incredible combination of chocolate, salty, sweet, and buttery flavors.

ACKNOWLEDGMENTS

From the time we met in culinary school until now, just about to open our first restaurant together, many people have influenced, changed, and molded our lives and careers into what they are today—too many people to thank individually, but here are a few individuals who made a real difference.

Frank Anderson, for always being on top of things in the kitchen and dealing with us on a day-to-day basis. It takes a very special person to do this job, and you do it very well. Your loyalty and efforts are invaluable.

Louis Gabriel, for letting us crash at the wood shop and start the company. You are the only person who knows how this all really got started. Thanks for your loyalty and believing in us. Your ideas, creativity, and craftsmanship are inspirational.

Michelle Bernstein, Kevin Kopsick, Doug Reese, Carl Donner, and Ray Roach. Without your influence and guidance in the kitchen we wouldn't be here today.

The Ford Family and Earl McGrath, for all of your support over the years, and for opening so many doors for us in Los Angeles.

Melissa Mathison, for keeping us alive in the beginning; your endless support and words of encouragement kept us going in the tough times.

Raquel Pelzel, for jumping onboard and really making it happen. You are a joy to work with. Your knowledge of food and writing skills made this a fun and easy project. Thanks for dealing with our crazy lives and schedules.

Kathryn Russell, for all of our beautiful photos and your patience and crew.

Meg Suzuki, for testing and adjusting all of the recipes.

Pam Krauss and her team at Clarkson Potter, including designer Jennifer K. Beal Davis, for being there from the start to listen to our crazy ideas and believing in us. We finally did it!

Lisa Shotland and her team at CAA, for making this deal happen and always listening to all of our problems.

Jeanne Newman and Candice and Barry Weiss, for keeping everything in line and always looking out for us and our best interests.

Food Network, for getting us out there on a mainstream level and believing in us.

To all of our present and past employees, for your contributions and efforts.

To all of our loyal clients, your support is what keeps us going.

INDEX

C

D